Brand
Name
Christians

••••••••••••••••••••••••••

A DEVOTIONAL FOR
JUNIOR HIGHERS

Brand Name Christians

MIKE WORLEY

Zondervan Publishing House
Grand Rapids, Michigan

BRAND NAME CHRISTIANS
Copyright © 1988 by Mike Worley

Published by Zondervan Publishing House,
1415 Lake Drive, S.E.,
Grand Rapids, Michigan 49506

Library of Congress Cataloging in Publication Data

Worley, Mike.
    Brand-name Christians: a Bible-study devotional for junior highers / Mike
Worley.
        p. cm.
    "Youth Books."
    Summary: A collection of devotions consisting of selected verses from four of
Paul's epistles paired with stories and questions related to their themes.
    ISBN 0-310-30291-9
    1. Bible. N.T. Epistles of Paul—Meditations—Juvenile literature. 2. Youth—
Prayer-books and devotions—English. [1. Bible. N.T. Epistles of Paul—Medita-
tions. 2. Prayer books and devotions.] I. Title.
BS2650.4.W67 1988
242'.63—dc19   88—1073
                                                                                    CIP

Printed in the United States of America

90 91 92 93 / CH / 10 9 8 7 6 5 4 3

To the men in my life whom God has used to help me be a *brand-name Christian*.

Don Worley—my dad, who always had time for me.

Mark Worley—my older brother, who has always been close to me.

Paul Worley—my younger brother, who has been a real friend.

Michael Worley—my son, who has brought more joy into my life than I could ever put into words.

Bob Pederson—my father-in-law, who encouraged me to write this book.

Jeff Pederson—my brother-in-law, who continues to make music to the Lord.

Ralph Peterson—my grandpa, who has been the best example a grandson could have.

Special thanks to my wife, Leesa, for being the most wonderful bride in all the world; my daughter, Katie, for the special place she has in my heart; my mother, Marrilyn, for always looking out for me; my mother-in-law, Betty, for her constant love, and to my grandma Peterson and grandma Worley who are busy enjoying the presence of the Lord. Special thanks also to Tammy Quigley for her dedication and time. Thanks to all of the young people of Los Gatos Christian Church who have captured my love and affection. I love you all.

WHAT'S IN THIS BOOK?

Philippians—A Trip Back in Time

1	2	3	4	5
6	7	8	9	10
11	12	13	14	15

Colossians—Unopened Letters

16	17	18	19	20
21	22	23	24	25
26	27	28	29	30

Ephesians—Good Morning?

31	32	33	34	35	36	37	38	39
40	41	42	43	44	45	46	47	48
49	50	51	52	53	54	55	56	57

Galatians—A Special Relationship

58	59	60	61	62	63
64	65	66	67	68	69
70	71	72	73	74	75

HOW TO USE THIS BOOK

Hi there, friend! My name is Mikey and I'll be spending the next seventy-five days with you in a very special way. No, we won't be riding the waves or shooting the curl—but we'll be doing something just as hot. Each day we'll open God's Word, the Bible, and read a few verses together. Then we will read a story, complete a puzzle, or answer a few questions. These next seventy-five days are going to be awesome!

What comes to your mind when you think of a brand name? Coca-cola? Guess? Levis? Reebok? No matter which brand name you think of, that name makes that product stand out from all the others. Brand-name labels appear on everything from jeans to soap to cereal boxes.

We have a special name, too. It is *Christian*—meaning a follower of Christ. That's a big name to live up to, but that's what we are if we have received Jesus Christ into our lives. *Brand-name Christians* stand out from other people because they have made Jesus Lord of their life. A *brand-name Christian* spends time in God's Word and really makes an effort to grow as a Christian. A *brand-name Christian* is serious about his or her relationship with Christ.

I want you to become a brand-name Christian too, my friend. I want to see you grow as you spend time in God's Word and apply it to your life. God made you just the way He wanted—but now He also wants you to *grow* in your Christian life.

And to help you become a brand-name Christian, we've designed this book to help you read God's Word, understand it, and apply it to your daily life. By the time you finish this book, you'll have read four books of the Bible! And once you start, believe me—you'll want to keep it up every day.

Here are four steps to complete each day. The whole thing will take you only ten or fifteen minutes—but it may be the best-spent time of your whole day!

1. Pray and ask God to speak to you. God *does* speak to us—through the Bible. You'll soon see how what the Bible says applies to you and your life. So let's start by asking God to help us out.

2. Read the Bible verses in the upper-left-hand corner, and then put a check mark in the space provided in the right-hand corner. Each day covers ten verses or less, so anybody can read it. If you can't find the book of the Bible you're looking for, just look in the table of contents of your Bible. Philippians, Colossians, Ephesians, and Galatians are all next to each other in your Bible, so once you find one you'll be real close to the others. *It will help you to use the New International Version of the Bible.* It's easy to read and understand, and it's the one I used in preparing this book. There are lots of other good translations of the Bible, but some parts of this book—such as the crossword puzzles—might be hard for you to understand if you use a translation other than the *New International Version.*

3. Read the story for the day. Some of these are funny and some are serious or sad. Take the time to read them, because I have some special things I want to share with you.

4. Fill in any blanks for the day. Some days I'll ask you a question, and some days you'll just put your thoughts into words.

Finishing all four of these steps will just take ten minutes or so, and they'll help you get the most out of this book and God's Word.

Know what? I sure love to surf! Each time I go surfing I pick a place where the waves will be forming well and a time when the tide will bring in the biggest ones. To start things off right, you need to pick a place and a time you are going to meet with me each day. For some of you it will be before school, and for others we will meet after school or before you go to bed at night. Be sure to pick the time and place that is best for you and jot it down below:

place _____

time _____

Good job, my friend! Now let's plan on meeting each day at the time and place you wrote down. Just to help you keep track of where you are in this book, I've included a chart on page 8 where you can cross off each day after you complete it—all the way up to seventy-five days.

We sure are going to have a good time together!

Looking forward to the next seventy-five days,

Mikey

A Trip Back In Time

Welcome to the
Book of Philippians

Let's travel back nearly two thousand years to visit a dark olive-skinned people, dressed in comfortable robes and leather sandals. Here the buildings are made of rough, gray brick, and the roads are dusty from the hot, dry weather and a warm breeze from the North.

Among the buildings we see a rather pleasant-looking one. But once inside, we begin shivering. A long, spiral staircase, made of stone, descends into a dark room. Listening to the sounds from there, we hear the groaning of men, whose physical strength has been completely drained by malnourishment and heavy chains, which strangle their wrists and ankles. Now we can also hear the faint squeaking of rats as they squeeze through the cracks and holes of the jail walls. We smell the sweaty bodies in this small, enclosed room. The smell is so bad that the guards leave immediately after their hourly check on the prisoners. Where are we? In a prison—a building, which represents punishment and death.

On the floor of this prison sits a little man with a pen in his hand. A small candle sheds a glimmer of light so he can write on the old yellow parchment. This short, baldish man resembles a man much older than his years. For you see, he has been through quite a lot in his life. He has been thrown into jail more times than he can remember and whipped on countless occasions, even faced death several times. Five times the Jews gave him thirty-nine lashes, and three times he was beaten with rods. Another time he was stoned and left for dead. Three other times he was shipwrecked in stormy seas and spent a whole night and a day drifting at sea before he was found. His feet show evidence of the many miles he has traveled through great dangers, from floods and robbers to irate Jews and Gentiles.

Watching him, we wonder what kind of words he would write—perhaps words of bitterness and regret. Maybe he is writing to get revenge upon those who have hurt him, but none of these are true. The precious words that were put on that old yellow parchment were words of love. He was writing a friendly letter of encouragement to those whom he considered his family. This man, Paul, was not a prisoner in chains, but free in Christ's love. Come and join me in discovering the truth of the words which came from that dark prison cell. Join me in a journey that you won't soon forget.

Your friend,

Mikey

★★ Day 1 ★★

Read Philippians 1:1–11   check here _____

The hardest part of model building is finishing it. Many model boxes have been opened up in excitement but found only partially built in the end.

One Christmas my brother and I each found a model of a car in our stocking. We were both pretty excited. The car on the cover of the box looked "bossanova." (That means it was rad.) We could each pic-ture that beautiful shiny car on top of our dresser before long.

Now Mark was a good model builder. He read the directions carefully, studied all the parts, patiently glued them together, and took whatever time was necessary to make his car look better than the one on the box. Soon, just as he imagined, that shiny car sat on top of his dresser.

On the other hand, I was good at starting a model project but rarely ever com-pleted it. You see, I was so busy pouring on the glue and putting on the stickers that I'd

forget to put parts together.

Usually my partially-completed projects soon found their way into the sights of my BB gun.

It's good to know that we are specially designed by God. He not only made us but also continues to complete His work within us through Jesus. When we ask Jesus into our lives, we become God's kids.

In our reading today, verse 6 promises us something. What does verse 6 say God will do with what He has started?

_____

Now that's hot! We aren't going to be left half-completed like some of my old models. He won't leave us alone and in the dark. God promises to always be there for us when we need Him. I don't know about you but I need Him every moment of every day!

Take a second and read verse 6 one more time. Put a check here ☐ when you have read it, then thank God for being with you as you grow as one of His special children. All of God's kids are under construction.

Happily under construction,

Mikey

Christians are always under construction.

★★ Day 2 ★★

Read Philippians 1:12–18   check here _____

Have you ever had the chance to tell someone that you go to church and that you are a Christian? Sometimes it is kind of scary to tell others that we are Christians, but the more we do it, the more confident we become.

When I was in seventh grade, my best friend's nickname was "Alfalfa." We called him Alfalfa because he looked just like Alfalfa on "The Little Rascals" television show. I remember telling Alfalfa about God many times during our long friendship. To my knowledge, my good friend never received Jesus Christ into his life. I felt like a failure because I wanted him to receive the gift of eternal life and walk with God each day, but he just wasn't interested.

Years later, I saw Kevin, Alfalfa's younger brother, in   15 church one Sunday, so I went over to say hello. As we sat down, Kevin told me that he used to follow Alfalfa and me around when he was a squirt. One day he overheard me explain how you just need to ask Jesus into your life and He will come in. Alfalfa didn't respond, but Kevin told me *he* went back into his room and asked Jesus to come into his life! He became a Christian that day, and he wanted me to know about it.

For over ten years I had thought my witnessing to Alfalfa was a waste, but it wasn't. I learned a valuable lesson: I do my part and God will do His. You see, you and I can't change a person's heart. Only God can do that. We need to share our life, our message, and our love with others but realize that *God* is One one who does the transforming work in their hearts. We are never failures, and our time is never wasted.

Paul always spoke to others, even while he was in jail. Who else knew that Paul was a Christian in verse 13? _____

_____.

Don't be afraid to admit that you are a Christian. You are special in the eyes of your heavenly Father and don't

16

forget it! Write down the name of someone you would like to invite to church next Sunday _____.

If you bring them, you're awesome!

Thankful that God does the work,

Mikey

The biggest task a Christian can do is to find his friend and introduce him to Jesus Christ.

★★ **Day 3** ★★

Read Philippians 1:19–30   check here _____

When I was seven years old, I asked Jesus Christ into my life. I was never a reformed drug addict or murderer but I certainly was a sinner! Even after Jesus came into my life, I did some real stupid things as a kid. I was in the growing process of learning to live like a Christian should.

One day I was in the garage with my brother when our gray and white cat came in. Now poor Tom just wandered into the garage looking for her water dish. She had no idea this little blonde kid was in a bad mood. Before Tom knew what hit her, I was swinging her in a circle by her tail. I really got a lickin' for that one and was reminded: live as a Christian should.

I also remember the day I took the paperboy's rubber bands and traded them for an aqua-green silhouette hot-wheel car. I again got a lickin' and was reminded—live as a Christian should.

I've grown up some now (thank goodness!), but I still need to be reminded that I need to live as a Christian should. A Christian means "Christ-one." How are you doing? Let's really try to live as Christians this week, O.K.?

What is the reminder in verse 27? _____

_____

Put verse 21 into your own words. _____

_____ **17**

Live as a Christian should. I'll be trying to do my best too!

Your buddy,

Mikey

Live as a Christian and you will shine as a light.

★★ **Day 4** ★★

Read Philippians 2:1–4   check here _____

You know, it sure is easy to be selfish; it comes naturally to all of us. Most of us tend to walk through life just caring about ourselves and our own needs. "We want it, we want it this way, and we want it now!" is a popular attitude (especially around home!).

In our local paper, there was a story about a man who was unselfish. He spent his time giving and helping other people, instead of just thinking of himself. He was one of the nicest men you could ever meet.

One day at a local lake, two kids were spotted in the water. They were splashing frantically and obviously drowning.

In an instant, an unidentified man jumped into the water and tried to swim to them—he couldn't swim well—in fact, barely at all. Soon the kids could touch him. I don't really know what happened next but I do know the two kids got to shore safely and the man didn't.

The next day his body was washed ashore. Yes, it was the nice man from town. Starting a professional football career, he was young and strong, yet not a bit selfish. Later his mother said that the young man didn't even know how to swim. He just wanted to help those kids.

According to Philippians 2:3, what attitude should we have? _____

What does Philippians 2:4 say we need to do? _____

_____

Don't be afraid to help someone today. In fact, write down two ways you can be helpful to someone today.

1. _____

2. _____

Looking out for others,

Mikey

There is nothing more pitiful than a life spent in thinking of nothing but yourself.

★★ Day 5 ★★

Read Philippians 2:5–11   **check here** _____

One day, in the kingdom of Sire, there arose a dispute. Many of the slaves and peasants gathered together at the drawbridge to the huge castle to address the king. Before long the king appeared on the balcony far above the slaves. He was adorned in purple robes and had a golden crown that sparkled in the early morning sunrise. His fingers were covered with jeweled signet rings of royalty. This king was a magnificent sight in all of his glory.

The slaves gathered below to voice their concern: "Oh gracious king, we are but mere slaves, but human beings just the same. For years in the kingdom of Sire we have been burdened with conditions unfit for human beings. We live under trees and in boxes we have made. We eat what berries we can find and the scraps of bread our masters give us. We are unjustly punished and treated worse than animals. We cannot live like this, our Majesty. Life has become unbearable."

Slowly, the slaves began to return to the forest as the king went back into the castle. "Our words have fallen on closed ears," muttered one of the slaves.

The next week the slaves were awakened by a rustling noise in the nearby forest. They grabbed their weapons and went to see what was happening. When they came to the area where they had heard the noise, they noticed a man lying on the ground. His worn clothes were hanging on his badly bruised and beaten body. His face was torn and swollen as was his freshly-beaten back.

"A slave from Sashire has fallen into the hands of our masters," said one of the slaves. "We must help him and keep him alive."

It took weeks for the stranger to regain his strength. He explained how he was captured near the Sire border and was beaten as a runaway slave. Before long each person was telling his own story of what it was like to be a slave in the land of Sire.

Soon the stranger was healthy enough to help work. His face was still badly bruised but he could carry water, work on the fences, and feed the livestock. The stranger became part of the little slave group until the day his bandages were taken off.

The old doctor came in and slowly began to unwind the dirty cloth from the stranger's sweaty face. The wounds had closed well and the stranger was allowed to wash the dirt and grime off his face. The doctor stood in amazement as the stranger turned around.

"This man, do you know who he is?" shouted the doctor. "Why, this is the king of Sire!"

The slaves stood in shock as they looked face-to-face with the king. For the last two months the king had shared their work, their food, and every aspect of their lives. He had become one of them to experience the seriousness of their problem. Now the masters in Sire would be different, and slaves would be given respect and eventual freedom.

The king of Sire couldn't have understood fully the problem of the slaves unless he became one of them. Read Philippians 2:5–11 one more time. This is one of my favorite passages because it tells how Jesus left His glory in heaven and became one of us and even died a criminal's death to free us from the disease of sin.

It doesn't end there, though. Take a look at 2:9–11. What is eventually going to happen?

That's right. *Every* knee shall bow and *every* tongue confess that Jesus Christ is Lord! Although we don't live in the kingdom of Sire, we do have a problem with sin. When was the last time you thanked Jesus for dying on the cross for your sins? Take a moment and do it right now.

Because of Jesus,

Mikey

He never rises high who does not know how to kneel.

★★ Day 6 ★★

Read Philippians 2:12–18　　　　check here _____

I once heard a story about a young boy in a remote village who had a problem with complaining. When he reached his teenage years, his complaining continued to grow. He became a real irritation to the village people and especially to those close to him. He consistently griped, grumbled, and was possessed with a negative attitude.

The village had a ceremonial rite when a boy became a man, and this boy's day had finally come. The village was all lit with torches; the ritual dances were performed in the usual way. After several hours the boy was brought before the chief. But instead of receiving the trademarks of manhood (a knife-carved design on the shoulder), the chief cut the boy's tongue out of his mouth!

"Now the boy can live in harmony with the rest of us," responded the chief.

I don't think you have to be worried about losing your tongue, but are you grumbling and complaining? A Christian can't be a light in the world if he has a negative attitude. Read 2:14—16 one more time. Why should we have a positive attitude?

Remember this the next time your parents ask you to do something!

From one light to another,

Mikey

If you think twice before you speak, you'll speak twice better for it.

★★ Day 7 ★★

Read Philippians 2:19–30   check here _____

Friends are special to each of us. A friend is a person who comes in when everyone else has gone out. A friend is someone who will always listen to you, always understand you, and always love you. When I asked Jesus into my heart at the age of seven, someone gave me the greatest advice I would ever hear: *"Make Jesus your best friend."*

Jesus is the one who will listen when no one else will. Jesus understands me even better than I understand myself and loves me more than I can humanly understand. We need to make sure that Jesus is our Lord and our friend.

A soldier recalled how he was running when all of a sudden a bullet pierced his shoulder. Several of his comrades circled around him, stood him up, and ran for cover. The wounded soldier never fell because his friends supported him from all sides. The next thing he remembered, he was sitting in a hospital bed.

22   Friends can support you at times, but there is no better

support than Jesus. In fact, turn to Matthew 11:28–30. What does Jesus say here to you? _____

_____

In today's reading, who were the two friends Paul mentions? _____

Take the time to talk to Jesus today. He wants to hear from you. Thank Him for your friends.

Your friend forever,

Mikey

Friends are friends forever, when the Lord's the Lord of them.

★★ **Day 8** ★★

Read Philippians 3:1–7   check here _____

In Paul's day, a bunch of people were claiming they were God's children, not because of their faith in the Lord Jesus Christ, but because of a tradition they had kept. They put their confidence in the laws and customs they followed, not the Lord Jesus Christ.

Paul points out that he fits their traditions—in fact, all of their criteria—perfectly. What are some of the qualifications he gave in verses 5 & 6?

1. _____

2. _____

3. _____

4. _____   **23**

Yet in verse 7, Paul says that all this doesn't matter in knowing Christ. It isn't a special cutting of the skin or being born into the right family that gets you into heaven; it *is* receiving Christ into your life.

I know people who think everything is okay in their relationship with God because they come to church once in a while. I know others who think they are "religious" because they have prayed. But you see, we can't do anything to work our way to heaven. That's what grace is—God's reaching down to man to provide salvation through Jesus' death for our sins. All we need to do is receive Him into our life, so that sin cannot separate us from Him. If you know someone in the "religious" category, try bringing them to church next Sunday.

Thinking of you,

Mikey

"Religion" is man working his way to God. A relationship with Jesus is God's reaching down to man.

★★ Day 9 ★★

Read Philippians 3:8–14   check here _____

I have a friend named Dave who runs marathons. A marathon is over twenty-six miles. Dave enjoys running (personally, I'd rather drive my car), but he says there is one point of the race he doesn't look forward to. Runners call this point in the race "hitting the wall," when a runner's body has given all that it can give and every bit of motivation for running is lost. Dave says the only thing you can think about is stopping and giving up. (I feel that way sometimes walking to the refrigerator.)

But this is the time when the runner's mind tries to take control and remind him that the finish line is just ahead. The runner's mind keeps him pressing and reaching forward one step at a time toward that glorious finish line. A runner who pushes himself through "the wall" and across that finish line has completed a great feat. He feels satisfied because he has given 110%. He has accomplished what he set out to do even if he didn't feel like doing it.

How does Paul describe his marathon with the Lord in verse 13? _____

_____

What does he press on toward in verse 14? _____

_____

Keep pressing on, my friend, even if you don't feel like it at times. I'll talk to you tomorrow!

In the race with you,

Mikey

Those who fail to press on never reach the finish line.

★★ **Day 10** ★★

Read Philippians 3:15–21   check here _____

Transformers are real popular toys nowadays. A kid can take a car, bend it several times, and the car turns into a person. Now that's pretty wild for a little boy.

Did you know that some day we are going to be transformed? No, we aren't going to turn into cars! Read verse 21 and write down what is going to happen to us. _____

_____

_____

Wow! We are going to have these earthly bodies changed into heavenly bodies—transformed into glorified bodies! We are talkin' major facelift here, folks.

25

What questions come to your mind about having a heavenly body? (I wonder if mine will be short?)

1. _____

2. _____

Whoever said the Christian life is boring doesn't understand the real Christian life. We have so much to live for and look forward to! I'm glad you read God's Word with me today. I'll see you tomorrow!

Living as a future citizen of heaven,

Mikey

The straight and narrow path is the only road that has no traffic problems.

★★ **Day 11** ★★

Read Philippians 4:1–3   check here _____

I am not the biggest guy in the world (5'4"). In fact, some people even think I am short! Can you believe that?

In high school some guy was breaking into the lockers while we were at P.E. He would search our wallets until he found some money, then leave. If anyone was coming in, he would be clued and not get caught.

One day the coach came to me and asked if I could help him. You see, up above the lockers was a tiny little room. The coach wanted me to wait in that tiny place and watch through a little hole he had made. He wanted the thief caught.

When everyone left the locker room the next day, the coach boosted me up to that little closet. I got inside and positioned myself so I could see out the little hole. After about twenty minutes, I heard a door close and in stepped this guy. He went to the lockers and began to open them. I looked at him for a while until I was sure that I could recognize him.

Later on that day, the coach called me into his office. I described the thief and he was soon apprehended. It felt good to nail that guy. Remember Batman's slogan, "Crime never pays."

Paul reminds us to stand firm in the Lord. We each need to stand up as a Christian and stand firm in what the Bible says. Think about that for a minute—did you stand firm today?

Standing firm in the Lord,

Mikey

People look at you six days a week to see what you mean on the seventh.

★★ **Day 12** ★★

Read Philippians 4:4–7   check here _____

Do you ever get anxious or worried about things? I do. What do you do when you get worried? Do you dwell on it and make things worse or do you do what Paul tells us to do? Paul reminds us to make our requests known to God. In other words, we should bug God with what bugs us! We do not have a God who just hangs around the cosmos. Instead we have a loving God who is concerned about each of us and wants us to call upon Him.

Prayer is special because God wants us to talk to Him. Sometimes taking the time to pray can change our day completely. Read this little poem.

THE DIFFERENCE

I got up early one morning
*   and rushed right into the day;*
I had so much to accomplish
*   that I didn't have time to pray.*

Problems just tumbled about me
   and heavier came each task;
"Why doesn't God help me?" I wondered.
   He said, "But you didn't ask."

I wanted to see joy and beauty
   but the day toiled on, gray and bleak;
I wondered why God didn't show me.
   He said, "But you didn't seek."
I tried to come into God's presence;
   I used all my keys at the lock.
God gently and lovingly chided,
   "My child, you didn't knock."

I woke up early this morning
   And paused before entering the day.
I had so much to accomplish
   That I had to take time to pray.
                    Author unknown

I know you have some things that are bothering you.
Write down three of them.

   1. _____

   2. _____

   3. _____

Now take some time and pray about each one. This is
how we make our requests known to God. What is the
promise in verse 7 if we do this? _____

_____

God loves you and wants to hear from you. When God
seems far away, guess who moved?

                              Praying with you,

                              Mikey

In heaven's calendar the most notable days are those
28 *when human prayers move the arm of God.*

★★ **Day 13** ★★

Read Philippians 4:8–9   **check here** _____

Your mind is very creative and powerful. It has the ability to create pictures and can help us in our walk with God. But used in the wrong way, our minds can be fed with sinful, destructive thoughts. Our minds can be used for our growth as Christians or our destruction. Let me illustrate.

When Eve was tempted in the garden, she *thought* about her situation before sinning. The serpent told her she would be like God if she ate from the tree. Eve *thought* about it, then sinned.

David was cruising along his balcony when he spotted Bathsheba. He *thought* about what it would be like to have her as his own. After he *thought* about it, he sinned.

Joseph was being tempted by his master's wife to shack up with her. He *thought* about how wrong it was and responded that he could not violate God's law and his master.

You see, before we sin a battle is waged in our minds. Many times the way we *think* about something causes us either to sin or not to sin. Today's passage reminds us to be careful about our thought life. God knows our very thoughts, and we need to keep them in line with our Christian walk. Wrong thoughts grieve God, and as His children we should be trying to please Him.

Paul reminds us to think on several things in verse 8. What are they?

1. _____

2. _____

3. _____

4. _____

5. _____

6. _____

7. _____

8. _____

We need to guard our thought life so we will be strong, as Joseph was. If we do not guard our thoughts, then sin is right around the corner. Ask God to help you have clean thoughts right now.

Thinking to please our King,

Mikey

Often, the thoughts to do ill make ill deeds done; therefore, avoid the thoughts!

★★ **Day 14** ★★

Read Philippians 4:10–13   check here _____

Paul learned a lot of different things when he was writing this letter to the Philippians. Can you find the six things Paul said he now knows? Every one of them begins with the word "I."

1. "I rejoice _____."
2. "I have learned _____."
3. "I know what _____."
4. "I know what _____."
5. "I have learned _____."
6. "I can do _____."

Now see if you can complete this puzzle. All the words are in verses 10–13.

Across
    1. Paul's attitude in v. 10.
    2. "I can do _____."
    3. Jesus is _____.
    4. A word that means a lot—v. 12.
    5. Another word for care—v. 10.

Down
    1. "_____ of being content."
    2. Paul was content in all _____. v. 11.
    3. 6th word in v. 10.

4. V. 12—"I have learned the secret of being content in _____ and every situation."
5. "_____ or hungry."

Learning with you day by day,

Mikey

Whether 7 or 70, Christians are growing and learning all the time.

★★ Day 15 ★★

Read Philippians 4:14–23   check here _____

Congratulations, my friend! You have just completed an entire book of the Bible. Good job! Now let's get ready to go through book number two—Colossians.

Some of you have never read a book of the Bible until now. I want you to know that I am really proud of you. It takes a lot of effort and discipline on your part to complete a section of this book, and you have done very well. Growing as a Christian won't happen until you read God's Word as you have been doing. You are growing, my friend!

Take a second and write down what day was your favorite as we read through the Book of Philippians. _____

Why was it your favorite? _____

Good job, buddy. Now let's get ready to read through the next book together. Keep up the great work. I am proud of you!

Meeting with you each day,

Mikey

Time in the Bible is time well spent.

Unopened Letters

Now We Are Off
to Colossians

They were hoping this day would never come but deep inside they knew that it would. They had been together for two years and were planning a wedding for next April. Everyone saw them as a very special couple and were excited about their future plans together.

But today was a different day. Dave was in the navy and was to report on the ship's deck by 5:00 P.M. He would be gone for eight months at sea and engaged in war.

Words could not express the sorrow and pain in each of their hearts as they said good-bye just before Dave stepped on deck. To be without the companionship of the one you love for eight months was indeed something that tugged at the depths of each of their hearts. They promised to write every day to each other, to be true to each other, and to wait for the other at the end of the long eight months. The tears flowed as the large naval ship slowly exited the harbor. Tammy stood lifeless and sobbing because a special part of her heart left with that ship. How could she go on living without the one she loved close to her? Only through the letters could she walk with him, so she sat down and began to write.

The letters came each week to Tammy's house. Her greatest thrill was to open the mailbox and recognize Dave's handwriting. As she read every detail of the letter, she tried to imagine the places he described and life on his ship. Tammy tried to bring those precious words to life because they were more than mere words on paper. They were somehow almost life-changing for her. She could be in a gloomy mood, but one of those letters would change that in an instant. After a couple of months, something happened.

Tammy went out to the mailbox and recognized one of Dave's letters. But instead of ripping into it, she tossed it on her desk and told herself she would read it later. That letter was the first of many that would never be opened. For some reason Tammy lost her excitement. Maybe receiving the

33

letters just became routine or maybe she just didn't feel like opening them. She still loved Dave but his letters were just collecting dust. All the thoughts and precious words he longed for her to read were never seen. His love, which he expressed so well, never was received.

Before long, the end of the eight months had arrived. Tammy went to the dock and watched her ship come in. Dave was one of the first sailors off the ship. They threw themselves into each other's arms for what seemed like hours.

"Did you get my letters?" asked Dave.

"Yes, I did," responded Tammy as she quickly changed the subject.

A few days later they were at Tammy's house when Dave sat at her desk and noticed one of his letters. It was unopened. He looked around the top of the desk and found several more letters. They, too, were unopened.

Tears began to fill his eyes as Tammy entered the room.

"What's the matter, Dave?" she asked.

Dave held up the unopened letters. Tammy looked down in shame. Dave couldn't understand why she hadn't opened the letters. Didn't she want to know him better? Didn't she long to find out how he was doing? Didn't she really love him?

Dave could barely speak around the lump in his throat.

"I wrote this one to you when I was suffering from malaria in a hospital. This one with the funny stamp on it was written by candlelight when enemy planes were above us. And this other one contains some treasured thoughts that I could not express to you in any other way. I don't know how you could say you love me and not even read my letters. How could you love me and not read my letters? My letters, my letters . . . "

If you were in love (and some of you may think that you are!), would you read the letters written to you? Of course, you would! You would read them again and again. You might even sneak your flashlight into bed with you and read them under the covers!

The greatest commandment in the Bible is for us to love the Lord with all of our heart, soul, and mind (Matt. 22:37). In
other words, we are to love God with all that we are and with

all that we have. But how can we love God if we don't read any of His love letters to us? How would you feel if the one you loved never opened the envelope but just pushed your letter aside, like Tammy? Many of us say we love God but very few of us open up His love letter. God has poured out His heart to us in a special collection of letters called the Bible, written so we can get to know Him better and to find out how He wants us to live.

Come and join me for the next fifteen days as we open these letters. Let's open up our hearts and discover God's special messages—written just for us!

★★ Day 16 ★★

Read Colossians 1:1–8   check here _____

There is a program that is seen and heard around the entire world. Up in the broadcaster's booth are men and women from every nation giving detailed descriptions in their native tongue. Everyone feels a bit more patriotic during these days. This event that catches the attention of the entire world happens only every four years. Do you know what it is? That's right, the Olympics.

The Olympics provide excitement for every corner of the globe and every corner watches to see if their Olympic hopefuls will bring home a medal.

What does Paul say about the gospel and the world in verse 6? _____

The message of Jesus is for every person in the world. It doesn't matter what color you are or how much money you   *35* have. It doesn't matter where you live or even what you have done. Christians are throughout the entire world. Although Christians are from every race and creed and from all backgrounds and upbringings, we are one through Christ. I am your brother; you are my brother or sister.

Your brother,

Mikey

If you belong to Jesus, you are part of the largest family on earth—the family of God.

★★ Day 17 ★★

Read Colossians 1:9–14   check here _____

I had a friend when I was just a kid named David. David and I were real good buddies, and as buddies often do, we liked to dare each other. One of us would say the other had to do something in order to be worthy of real friendship.

I'll never forget one day when David dared me. He said that I had to go up on his roof with an umbrella and jump off (like the guys in "Mary Poppins"). Now you have to understand that this was a big dare. I mean I was used to being dared into riding my bike with no hands or running down a hot asphalt street without shoes on, but to jump off a roof with an umbrella?!

Then came those unforgettable words from David. "Hey Mike, I double-dare ya!"

Now I had heard of being double-dared before but never had actually experienced it. I mean, Darnell Billingsly was double-dared to touch a bee hive once, and his face looked like a water balloon for weeks! To this day I still can't believe David dared me to do that.

In verse 10, Paul is praying, and he reminds us to live a life worthy of the Lord. (I'm so happy He doesn't double-dare us!) What are the four phrases that follow in verse 10 that help us walk worthy of the Lord?

1. _____

2. _____

3. _____

4. _____

Now pick one you can work on today and write it below.

Have a great day, my friend!

Mikey

To please the Lord is to walk with Him each day.

P.S. You probably are wondering if I jumped off that roof with the umbrella. Well, let me put it this way. My little friend thought I was real brave, and he never double-dared me again.

★★ **Day 18** ★★

Read Colossians 1:15–17   **check here** _____

A little boy was playing in the family room with some of his toys. A fire was blazing in the fireplace, and Dad was in his chair reading the newspaper. As the boy circled his toy trucks around the carpet, he asked his dad a question that only a young boy could ask.

"Dad, what does God look like?"

Dad began to squirm a little in his big chair. He set down his paper and saw those big blue eyes lovingly awaiting the answer. After all, Dad was always right.

Dad took a second to think and then responded as only a tender-hearted father could.

"Well, son," he began, "we don't know exactly how God looks. But close your eyes for a minute and picture in your mind what I tell you. Picture two eyes that watch with excitement as you play in the yard and yet cry with you when you get hurt. Think of a warm smile that tells you you're the most important little boy in the world. There are two strong hands that clap for you when you do good things and gentle arms that wrap themselves around you when you need a hug. His legs would keep right in step with yours because He cares for you and doesn't want to see you get far from Him. He would be everything that is good and perfect, my son. His face would tell you that He loved you without even speaking a word. If He did speak a word, it would always be something nice about you. Now open your eyes and tell me what you saw."

The little boy had a big warm smile on his face from picturing what God must look like.

"God must look just like you, Dad," he said.

Dad sat almost paralyzed from those precious words. He could feel his heart beginning to melt as his son jumped into his lap and gave him a hug. Dad hung onto that hug for a long time. Long enough for his tears to make their way off his cheeks.

Today's passage centers on the person of Jesus. The Bible tells us that *He* is the image of the invisible God. He has always been and always will be. To get a picture of God, we must look closely at the life of our Lord Jesus. Soon, the invisible God becomes visible to us.

What did Jesus do for us? (vv. 13–14) _____

_____

Whom is Jesus the image of? (v. 15) _____

What do verses 16–17 say to you? Put it in your own words below. _____

_____

These verses may raise a few questions. If you have a question or two, write them down right here:

1. _____

2. _____

I am really proud of you. It looks like we are going to have a great week together. Keep it up every day!

Loving our Father with you,

Mikey

Jesus is the exact representation of our heavenly Father.

★★ Day 19 ★★

Read Colossians 1:18–20   check here _____

The few verses we read today center on the person of Jesus Christ, don't they? In fact, verse 18 says that Jesus is the head of the body, so that in everything He might have supremacy. What does the word supremacy mean to you? __

_____

Now go ask one of your parents what supremacy means and jot it down here. _____

_____

Another word for supremacy is lordship. Lordship means to have first place in everything. Do you think Jesus wants to be Lord of your life? Sure He does! When we put Him first, we truly honor Him in our lives. That's what it takes to be a brand-name Christian!

Is Jesus Lord of your life? Here's a quick test. Which picture *best* represents you? The one with you on the throne or the one with Jesus on the throne?

If you need to, pray and put Jesus back on the throne today and then read this poem.

ONE LIFE

He was born in a stable
In an obscure village,
From there He traveled
Less than 200 miles.

He never won an election,
He never went to college,
He never owned a home,
He never had a lot of money.

He became a nomadic preacher, but
Popular opinion turned against Him,
He was betrayed by a close friend,
And His other friends ran away.

He was unjustly condemned to death, then
Crucified on a cross among common thieves
On a hill overlooking the town dump.
When dead, He was laid in a borrowed grave.

Nineteen centuries have come and gone,
Empires have risen and fallen,
Mighty powers have marched,
And powerful rulers have reigned.

Yet no one has affected men as much as He,
He is the central figure of the human race,
He is the Messiah, the Son of God,
*   JESUS CHRIST.*

"He is the image of the unseen God,
And the first-born of all creation,
For in Him were created all things,
In heaven and earth." Col. 1:15—16

Kristone

Jesus was not just a man. He was God in human form! Has His life changed yours? I hope so. Keep living for the Lord and put a smile on your face!

Never the same because of Jesus,

Mikey

When we recognize Jesus' Lordship, we'll give Him our worship.

★★ **Day 20** ★★

Read Colossians 1:21–23   check here _____

He was eleven years old and had never met his father. For three years Lance got up at 4:15 A.M. so he could begin folding papers for his early morning route. He had been saving every penny in hopes of this big day.

Lance rode his bike to the office building and took the elevator to the third floor. He opened the door to "Suite A" and asked to see Detective Peterson. Detective Peterson greeted the boy and asked him what he wanted.

"Sir," Lance said in a respectful voice, "here is three year's worth of money from my paper route. I hope it's enough because I want you to find my father."

"Do you understand that we are not very successful in most of these cases, son?" asked the detective.

"Yes, sir, but I have checked, and you have the best record of anyone in this city. I am willing to put my confidence completely in you. Will you please try to find my father so we can be together?"

The detective counted the money. Yes, it would cover the bills and yes, he would try to find the boy's father.

Several weeks passed with no word from the detective. Then one day the phone rang. It was the detective, and he wanted Lance to come down right away.

Lance hopped on his bike and headed downtown. *He must have found something*, thought Lance as he peddled along.

As he entered the detective's office, Lance noticed the shadow of a strange man sitting in the corner. He had never seen the stranger before in his life.

"Well, what did you find, detective?"

"It took several weeks, young man, but I think I found something."

The detective's eyes glanced over toward the stranger sitting in the chair.

Lance slowly moved over to the chair and looked into the stranger's eyes. They were warm and had a familiar look to them. His hair was thinning but had the same style as Lance's.

"Are you my father, sir?" asked Lance in a shaky voice.

The man stood up slowly and began to speak.

"Eleven years ago I was separated from my wife and my baby boy when our ship began to sink. I thought they were dead with the rest. The reports had them missing and presumed drowned. My searching led me nowhere.

"Then, Detective Peterson found me. He told me your story and showed me pictures."

Tears began to fill the man's eyes.

"Lance, I am your father."

At that, Lance jumped into his arms and cried tears that had been bottled up for years. He was together with his father again, never to be separated.

Does verse 21 say that we were separated from God at one time? _____

What has brought us back together with God again? (v. 22) _____

Yes, Jesus paid it all. Take a minute and thank Jesus today.

Because of Jesus,

Mikey

Jesus made it possible for all of us to be home with God.

★★ Day 21 ★★

Read Colossians 1:24–29   check here _____

Many years ago in a small Swiss village, there was an auction. All the people from the surrounding villages and towns came to this big event. Everything from saddles to furniture was sold at the auction, and everyone took part in it.

One of the items up for sale was an old violin. It was very old, and its strings were tired and out of tune. Its body was rough and worn. The violin even had a funny shape to it because it had been warped by the sun. This old violin had been collecting dust for years, and it surely wouldn't bring much of a price at the auction.

Before long the violin was up for sale. The auctioneer began to chatter out a price starting at one dollar. No one responded until finally a little old man emerged from the crowd. He held up his hand and purchased the worthless violin for a mere dollar.

As he paid his dollar, he asked if he could use the platform for a moment. The auctioneer moved aside, and the little old man took his place on the stage. Before the large crowd, this master musician began to tune the old violin. Then, he played one of the most moving works of music that had ever been played. The crowd was spellbound as the master musician brought life out of the old stringed instrument. Time seemed to stand still as the beautiful music filled the air.

When the little old man had finished, the crowd went wild. They had never heard such wonderful music before. They screamed and cheered for more tunes to be played.

The master musician then asked if anyone would like to buy the old violin. The people began to holler prices.

"Fifty dollars! Sixty! Make it seventy-five!"

Before long the little instrument was sold for $115. By itself, the old violin wasn't worth much. But once it was in the master's hands, the price soared, and the value of that stringed instrument skyrocketed.

We, too, are priceless in the Master's hands. God can take the simplest person and make something beautiful out of his life. He is the Master Musician just waiting for you to give Him a chance with your life. Will you allow Him to use you this week? Will you be sensitive to Him as you walk down the corridors of your school? Give the Master Musician control of your life, and let His music be played through you!

Can you tell me what Paul's goal was in verse 28? _____

That's my goal for you, too. I want to see you grow complete in Christ.

Letting the Master Musician have control,

Mikey

Sweet music can come from any instrument if the Master Musician is in control.

★★ **Day 22** ★★

Read Colossians 2:1–5   check here _____

Like crossword puzzles? Here's one. All answers are found in Colossians 2:1–5. Good luck!

Across

1. "So that they may have the full riches of complete
_____."
2. "Not there"—v. 5
3. Paul's attitude in v.5 about their orderly conduct.
4. Same as 4 down.
5. Paul's purpose—encouraged in _____.
6. Opposite of empty.
7. Author of Colossians—my brother's name.
8. Word #74 beginning with "I" in 2:1.
9. The name of this book of the Bible.
10. Opposite of flabby.

Down

1. The city mentioned in 2:1.
2. In whom are all treasures?
3. Some were deceived by these.
4. 2nd word in v. 2.
5. Paul was doing this for them.
6. All had not met Paul this way.
7. "Treasures of _____.
8. "_____ of wisdom & knowledge."
9. The Lord Jesus _____.
10. Opposite of empty.

Good job, my friend. I'll talk to you tomorrow.

Filled with Jesus,

Mikey

Jesus has all the pieces to the puzzle of life.

★★ **Day 23** ★★

Read Colossians 2:6–15   **check here** _____

Two men were in a dark prison cell awaiting the day of
their release. One was guilty of stealing some fruit and meat
from the market place. He had hoped to feed his three
children in the nearby alley.

The other man was thrown into prison on false charges.
He was going to a Bible study meeting when he saw a man

run recklessly out of the bank. He dropped his books and trailed the robber in hot pursuit. As he turned a street corner, he felt a painful crash upon his head, and everything went black. The police saw him running and thought he was the robber. Without questions being asked, he was thrown into prison.

On the same day, both men were brought up before the judge. The first man was read his certificate of debt. He was to work in the dreaded coal mines for two long years. The man stood in absolute shock as the judge read the horrifying decree.

The second man was granted a pardon. In fact, the department was to pay the man $1,000 in reward money because of his valiant efforts.

As the handcuffs were unlocked, the man asked about Ordinance 351. The officer looked shocked as he understood what was about to happen. You see, Ordinance 351 was a special clause allowing one prisoner to take the place of another. It was rarely used. I mean, who would want to be put back into prison or sent back to the terrifying coal camps upon release?

The second man was brought before the superior judge and soon was sent back to prison. The first man was released and, according to Ordinance 351, received the $1,000 reward. He left for home that night; the second man was sent to the coal camp to begin his two-year stay.

Several months later, the free man went to visit his fellow prisoner at the coal camp. Before long a man emerged soaked in sweat and covered with coal dust.

"Why did you do what you did, my friend?" asked the man who stood on the free side of the electric fence.

"I was guilty once, too, and headed for hell, until someone took my place. Jesus took all of my sins and nailed them to the cross. I will never be the same again. I just wanted you and your family to understand His love for you. The most important decision in your life now awaits you. Will you accept Jesus and His sacrifices for your sins or will you ignore it?"

Tears filled the guilty man's eyes as he realized his need for the Savior. That same day he and his family became Christians.

This little story came from verse 14. We had a certificate of debt consisting of wrongs we had done. Jesus took it and nailed it to the cross. Read verse 14 again.

How many of our sins are forgiven? (v. 13) _____

Thank Him for taking your place.

Because He took my place,

Mikey

Many have entered God's kingdom because one man took their place.

★★ Day 24 ★★

Read Colossians 2:16–23   check here _____

One of the special joys of a father is being able to pass his name through a son. The Worley name has been passed down through several generations as fathers have had sons to pass the name onto. When Michael was born, there was a special excitement in my own heart because I knew the Worley name would live on through another generation.

A name is something very precious. Your parents gave you a first name—one that fits only you. Others may have the same name but to your parents you are the only one that counts with the name they gave you. Some day you will be able to decide on a name for your son or daughter. It will be a very special time as you decide his or her name.

When a woman is married, she takes upon herself a new transformation. She is given a new name—her hus-   47 band's. It took Leesa quite a while to get used to being Leesa Worley instead of Leesa Pederson. I mean she was called Leesa Pederson for over eighteen years! In just one day, she took on a different name for the rest of her life.

Names are special. Here is a poem about how a father passes on his last name to his son. Before you read it, look at Proverbs 22:1. Read it slowly three times and grasp its meaning. Then read this poem.

YOUR NAME

You got it from your father, 'twas
the best he had to give.
And right gladly he bestowed it. It's
yours, the while you live.
You may lose the watch he gave you
and another you may claim,
But remember, when you're tempted,
to be careful of his name.
It was fair the day you got it, and
a worthy name to bear,
When he took it from his father,
there was no dishonor there.
Through the years he proudly wore
it, to his father he was true,
And that name was clean and spotless
when he passed it on to you.
Oh, there's much that he has given
that he values not at all.
He has watched you break your playthings
in the days when you were small.
You have lost the knife he gave you
and you've scattered many a game,
but you'll never hurt your father
if you're careful with his name.
It is yours to wear forever, yours to
wear the while you live.
Yours, perhaps, some distant morning,
another boy to give.
And you'll smile as did your father
—with a smile that all can share.
If a clean name and a good name you
are giving him to wear.

Edgar A. Guest

What kind of name will you pass on?

I love that poem! When we sin we not only hurt ourselves and others but we can dirty the precious name our parents gave us. Think about your name—are you making others proud of it or are you bringing disgrace to it? What do others think of when they hear your name? Live up to your name today.

You are special to me, my friend. Thanks for being just the way you are.

Mikey

As Christians we have a big name to live up to.

★★ Day 25 ★★

Read Colossians 3:1–4   check here _____

Once upon a time there was a caterpillar named Clarence. Clarence was your average little crawly critter. He had hundreds of little legs, fuzzies covering his whole body, and two eyes that bulged out of his little head. He had the usual black and orange colors, too. Clarence was an average caterpillar.

Clarence moved very slowly as most caterpillars do. Several of his front legs would move and then several of his back legs would run to catch up. This action caused a continual "hump" motion as Clarence walked along. He **49**

could climb trees, bushes, and even houses. Old Clarence thought he was pretty big stuff.

One day Clarence became extremely tired. He thought he must be getting real sick because he had a strong desire to hang upside down and sleep. Now this was strange for a caterpillar. So Clarence climbed to a high branch, hung upside down, and began a nice, long nap.

When Clarence woke up, he felt really strange. Everything was dark, and it seemed like he had been asleep for weeks. He felt different somehow but he couldn't put his finger on it. As Clarence tried to move, he began to realize that he was in some kind of a cage. Clarence knew he needed to get out because it was getting hard to breathe.

With great force Clarence began to stretch the walls of the cage. It took all of his might to put pressure on those walls. Finally, after hours of struggling, one of the walls cracked. Soon another wall cracked and before long the cage was broken to pieces.

Clarence was still hanging upside down when he realized that he still felt very strange.

"I need to stretch these tired muscles," he thought.

Slowly he began to stretch and to his amazement, a miracle unfolded. Bright colored wings were attached to his little body, and as he stretched, these new wings of his expanded in amazing brilliance.

"What a nap," responded Clarence. "I go to sleep a caterpillar and wake up a beautiful butterfly. I wonder what will happen if I take another nap. Maybe I'll turn into a bird!"

Just then Clarence heard the laughter from the old owl.

"You won't turn into anything else," responded the wise owl. "But you will need to get a new perspective on life. You see, you will no longer climb up trees, bushes, or houses. Instead, you will fly above them. You will no longer crawl across the ground, but you will dance in the air and rest upon flowers. You will need to think differently now, Clarence. You must set your mind on the things above, for you are a new creature now."

Clarence, realizing he had died to his old self, took off into the air as a new-born creature. His life would never be the same again.

Read Colossians 3:1–4 one more time. Now turn to 2 Corinthians 5:17 and write it in your own words right here.

_____

You see, we are kind of like Clarence. We are new creatures in Christ. Because we are new creatures, we need to get a new perspective on life. Colossians 3:1 says we need to seek what? _____

_____

_____

Verse 2 tells us to set our mind on what? _____

_____

_____

Yes, we have died to our old sinful self and have now put on Christ in our lives. What's the promise in verse 4? ____

_____

_____

Let's have a great week, and hey, if you see a caterpillar, don't step on him!

Reborn in Christ,

Mikey

Citizens of heaven need to focus on kingdom activities.

★★ Day 26 ★★

Read Colossians 3:5–11   check here _____

When something is dead, there is no feeling, no emotion, and no response left in its body. The once sensitive body is now lifeless and does not respond to the touch of another. When something is dead, its earthly life has come to an end.

In today's passage we are told to be dead to sin. In other words, we are to be so radically different from this   51 world that we become lifeless when it comes to sin. When temptation knocks on our door, we are to turn the other way. When sin tries to trip us, we are to set our sights on Jesus and become dead to that sin. You see, we don't want sin to have an effect on our lives anymore.

What does verse 6 say? _____

_____

What is the command in verse 9? _____

_____

Let's be dead to sin this week at school and in our free time. Live your life before the Lord, and put on the new self that this chapter talks about. I'll be praying for you as you seek to honor the Lord with your life. You are special just the way you are!

Putting on the new self,

Mikey

In order to hate sin, you need to love God!

★★ Day 27 ★★

Read Colossians 3:12–17   **check here** _____

Don't rush through this passage today. It is full of truth and warnings that we need to follow. Let's look at a few things that we could apply to our lives today. Most of you have dissected a grasshopper, worm, or frog in biology class. But have you ever dissected a verse from the Bible? Come on, let's start slicing this puppy up! (oops!)

VERSES 12–13

Who is the verse talking to? _____

What should our heart be full of?

1. _____

2. _____

3. _____

4. _____

What should you do if you have a complaint against someone? _____

If we just read a verse, we miss all this meaty stuff. Take the time to probe a little bit and find the phrase that applies to you and your life.

VERSE 14

What should we put on beyond all others? _____

Why? _____

See, there are some beefy tidbits of truth here. Now look at verses 15, 16, and 17. Write down two insights from each verse. It doesn't have to be some earth-shattering answer but just something that stands out as you read it.

VERSE 15

1. _____

2. _____

53

VERSE 16

1. _____

2. _____

VERSE 17

1. _____

2. _____

Now that wasn't so bad, was it? When we take the time to really dig into God's Word, we come out of it a little bit different. The Word of God really has an effect on our lives if we read it and follow it.

Reading His Word with you,

Mikey

Thy Word is a lamp unto my feet, and a light unto my path.

★★ **Day 28** ★★

Read Colossians 3:18–25

check here _____

Long, long ago, our Heavenly Father decided He would create a being in His image. He would call him man and his partner woman. They would come together and bear children. The father and mother and children would share a special relationship together, closer than any other relationship—a relationship in which they would be loved and would give love. After many years, the children would be old enough to seek a partner of their own with whom to continue that special union. This relationship, one of the most treasured of all, is the family.

I hope you can look and see warmth, love, and Christlikeness in your family. Within your family you can always share a smile, always dream a dream, and always find love. As you read this, think about your own special family.

YOUR FAMILY

Our family is a blessing
It means so many things
Words could never really tell
The joy our family brings
Our family is mutual love
The love of dad and mother
Showing children how to love
And care for one another
Our family is heartfelt pride
The feeling deep and strong
That makes us glad to take a part
And know that we belong
Our family is always home
A place where we can share
Our joys and sorrow, hopes
And dreams
For happiness lives there
Our family is a bond of faith
that even time can't sever
A gift to last throughout our lives
The family of God is forever
Kristone

What family relations are discussed in verses 18–25? Write down here every time a member of the family is mentioned. _____

_____

Now take a minute and pray for each member of your family. They may not be perfect, and you may not always see eye-to-eye, but take time to pray for each of them right now.

I'm glad you are a part of my family,

Mikey

Let your home face toward the Father's house.   55

★★ **Day 29** ★★

Read Colossians 4:1–9   check here _____

Have you ever invited someone to come with you on a Sunday morning or weeknight meeting? Did they come with you? Here are a few actual remarks of people who have been brought by a friend to our group meetings.

"I've never laughed like that at a church before."

"I didn't know you could have fun at church."

"That one guy is real short."

"I think this guy knows me because what he said really made sense to me."

"I have never seen so many junior highers come to a church before."

We all have preconceived ideas of what "church" is like. A lot of your friends picture a few kids sitting in chairs with their hands folded and some old bald guy boring them to death. That is called a stereotype. We need to invite our friends so they can see what the Christian life is all about. They need to hear the message of Christ, and they need a chance to receive Christ into their lives. Will they ever hear this message? A lot of that depends on *you*.

How does verse 5 relate to witnessing? _____

_____

What does verse 6 say about what you speak? _____

_____

_____

When you are walking through the hallway at school, ask that friend to go with you to church. Even offer to pick him or her up! A little act of kindness can result in your friend's accepting Christ. Take time to share, my friend.

Sharing Christ with others,

Mikey

Let your life speak for Christ, but be careful that your lips are not silent.

★★ Day 30 ★★

Read Colossians 4:10–18   check here _____

I want to congratulate those of you that have completed all of this devotional to here. It takes a lot of discipline and hard work, and I am really proud of you. You are about halfway through this book now!

Those of you who did not finish all of these but still did a bunch, need to understand that you did a great job, too. We all need to put forth effort in our relationship with the Lord. I am really proud of all of you, and I praise God for what He is doing in your young lives! Keep up the walk!

Today is my younger brother's birthday. He is very special to me, and I want to share something he wrote to my wife, Leesa, on her birthday:

> *As I sit at my window looking out upon the world*
> *I notice the landscape being swallowed up by the haze,*
> *as a squirrel hops along the fence.*
> *The hills are full of mystery*
> *while lights dance upon them giving traces of houses,*
> *protecting those inside from the elements.*
> *Children scamper through the park*
> *trying to get in a few last moments of play time*
> *before darkness ends their day.*
> *I remember days of endless fun in that park,*
> *with my brothers.*
> *I thought it would go on forever.*
> *But they grew up and I remained a child.*
> *I couldn't understand why they would want a girl,*
> *instead of me.*

57

I started understanding after I watched you
with my playmate.
You made him shine.
There was something you had I didn't.
I tried to stay jealous,
then I got to know you.
You made me shine, too.
We became good friends
when the one we had in common
left to go to school.
I don't know who missed him more
you or me.
My jealousy had diminished completely
by the time you took his hand,
and our name.
While you were away with him,
I found myself missing you
as well as him.
My world was back to normal when he came back
with you by his side.
As time went by
I sometimes asked you for advice
instead of him.
You then truly became as one
when you bore him not just a baby,
but a son.
I watch you from a silent distance
keeping track of both your boys.
I now realize that my brother
made the right choice,
when he chose you,
as his wife
and the mother of his son.

Paul Sheridan Worley, 1985

My wife and I love my younger brother. He is special to us beyond words. If you have a brother or sister, share a smile with them today.

Your brother in Christ,

Mikey

Brothers and sisters are only at home with us for a 58 *short time—remember to enjoy your time with them.*

Good Morning?

Introduction to Ephesians

The alarm goes off; you drag your body out of bed. For some reason this seems to be the most difficult part of your day. The piercing sound of that dumb alarm irritates you because it reminds you that the shower is waiting. As you start sudsing, you notice that the Coast soap doesn't wake you up as the television commercial promises.

"Irish Spring would have been better," you growl as you reach for your towel, only to find it not there.

As you try to wash your hair, the Vidal Sassoon styling shampoo is stuck in the unbreakable bottle. Then when you blow-dry your hair, everything flops when it should have flipped! You could tell it was going to be one of those days.

After you stumble out to the breakfast table, you pour the Lucky Charms into your bowl. With each spoonful, you glance up and read the ingredients on the side of the box and the proof of purchase seal. Next comes the best part of breakfast. You turn the back of the box of cereal toward you and read about how you can win a Winnebago motor home or an Atari if you enter the Luckyhead Luck-o contest. Soon the last yellow moon, green clover, and pink heart disappear. You grab your books, tell your mom good-bye, and leave for school. It looks like just another average day in the life of a junior higher.

But something seems wrong. You see, this person is a Christian and Jesus is *supposed* to be the most important person in his life.

Will you spend any time with God today? I wonder how the Lord feels knowing that we put more time into reading the back of a cereal box or a shampoo bottle than His Word?

Are you ready for the next book, my friend? If you just put forth a little effort, I really believe that God's Word will begin to change your life. Our greatest need is to know God in a close, personal way and become more like Him. If we take the time to get to know God and to love Him, then our lives will be transformed from the inside out. Let's let God make us into what He wants us to be. What do you say? **59**

In junior high we experience a busy and confusing world. It's easy for us to forget about God and live as if He doesn't even exist. But God *does* exist and He *does* care about you. He tells us He loves us through His creation, His Son, and His special love letters to us. Getting to know God through His Word will affect every area of your life. Come on. Let's open the pages that follow and continue a special walk with God together.

★★ Day 31 ★★

Read Ephesians 1:1–6   check here _____

The little baby boy had been found in the forest by a poor peasant woman. She had been out picking berries when she heard a cry coming from behind a large bush. There, in a basket, cried a baby no more than a few weeks old. He was wrapped well and had something hanging around his neck. The peasant woman looked closely at the ring attached to the necklace the baby was wearing. It was made of gold and even had two jewels in it. She took the ring and slipped it into her pocket so no one would steal it. She would have to find a safe hiding place for it later. Then she took the baby and headed for her humble home.

Peasants lived in poverty in those days, so the baby grew up in a dusty old shack. His toys were just pieces of wood that a friend had carved and rocks that were found outside. As time went by, he made friends in the village and could be seen playing outside all the time.

Then one day his mother became very ill. She had a high fever and lost her strength quickly. She remained this way for several days. There was hardly a moment when the boy wasn't by her side wiping her brow with a wet cloth. He knew his mother was slipping away from this life and into the next.

He was sitting by her side when all of a sudden she reached out and put her hand on his.

"I must tell you something, my precious son," she said in a hoarse voice. "Many years ago I was out in the forest picking berries when I heard the cry of a baby. I looked behind a bush and found this little child wrapped up in a blanket. That little child was you, my son. At the time I found you, there was a necklace with a valuable ring around your neck. Go get it in the third earthen jar."

The boy ran over to the familiar jar and found the ring near the bottom of it. He then rushed over to his mother's side.

"This ring is yours, my son. With it I believe you can find who your real family is. Go and find them. Always remember me and the things I have taught you. I love you, and remember I always will."

With those last words the boy's mother slowly lost her grip of his hand and was soon gone from this life.

The young boy wept in grief and pain for hours. The sorrow was more than he could bear. The words of his mother echoed in his young mind. She wished for him to find his real parents, and this is what he set his mind to do.

The twelve-year-old boy departed early the next morning. He carried enough food for a week and a few blankets to use for his bedding. With determination, he headed north into an unknown world.

Two days into his journey, the boy came to a small village. He went over to rest his horse and grab a cup of warm soup. As he dropped off his horse, the stable master noticed his ring.

"It is an honor to have you here, sire. Ask whatever you wish and I will be quick to complete the task."

The boy stood puzzled. "Can you just feed my horse a little?" he asked in a kind voice.

"I will do so at once. Please come into my humble home and share a meal with us and rest a bit. We would be honored to have you come into our home."

The boy smiled and graciously accepted the stablemaster's offer. He had never been treated with such respect and loyalty. He would find out why he was treated so well at dinner.

Throughout the meal the boy was waited on like a king. He stuffed his empty stomach and then sat back in his chair.

"Sir, I wish to ask you a question. What does this ring mean to you?"

The stablemaster bowed with respect as he answered.

"The ring signifies your nobility in the kingdom of Naptolia. You are the heir to the kingdom and all respect you."

The boy sat in shock as he realized his true heritage and who his parents were. He had heard stories in the village of the king and how his son had been taken from the castle one night. Now he began to put the pieces together. He was that son!

With a bow of thanks, the boy shot out the door, jumped on his horse, and galloped to the Naptolia castle. He came upon the castle just before nightfall and asked to see the king.

Before long he was brought before the king and queen.

"What is your business?" bellowed the king.

"My business is to declare who I am—your son."

The king sat up a little and laughed. "Boys your age come by daily and pester us about our son who was taken from us. When will you leave us alone? You have no proof!"

"With all due respect, sire, I am different from all of the others. You see, my mother found me in the forest twelve years ago with this ring around my neck. It is your ring, king of Naptolia."

The king and queen jumped out of their seats to examine the ring. It was the king's ring. They studied him for a while, and tears began to fill their eyes. Yes, this was their son. This was the son who would inherit all of Naptolia. He would live in the castle, eat the finest of foods, and wear the most elegant clothes. This son would ride the finest horses in the land and be the richest man in all of the known world.

All of this, and for most of his life he hadn't even known it.

Ephesians 1:3 says something about you and spiritual blessings. What does it say? _____

_____

That's right, my friend. God has blessed us in many ways, and at times we live as if we don't even know it.

Can you write three blessings you have inherited since becoming a Christian?

1. _____

2. _____

3. _____

(Here's some help: John 5:24, Heb. 13:5, John 16:13, Rev. 21:4, Ps. 37:4, Rom. 8:1–2, Rom. 5:19).

Counting my blessings with you,

Mikey

As one of God's kids, you have the greatest inheritance ever given.

★★ Day 32 ★★

Read Ephesians 1:7–14   **check here** _____

SUMMER TROUBLES

The air was hot and muggy on this boring day in August. Johnny Quest and the Bugs Bunny Show had just ended, and David and I had nothing to do. After a bowl of sugar-frosted flakes, we hopped out of our light pajamas and struggled into our clothes. We went into the dining room and attached all the fluorescent Hot Wheels tracks we had to the big alarm clock. After several runs, we were bored and looked for something else to do.

We headed into the garage and jumped into our car. I was the race car driver, and David was the pit crew. After rearranging the hubcaps and adjusting the mirrors several times, the race began. I pumped the gas pedal for several minutes and made some great hairpin turns, then I accidentally hit the horn. The race ended when my dad came out of the house and screamed at us. He said something about flooding. I couldn't understand that, because it wasn't even raining. I looked at him strangely and left the race—disqualified.

Soon, David and I were in the side yard. We were sitting on the ground and telling each other whose dog was better than the others when an idea popped into my head. Rising above us was the Robertson's chimney. With both of our minds strategically at work, we each picked up a pebble.

"You first," David said.

"Chicken," I snapped as I sent the pebble toward the chimney.

CLING!

"I hit it! I hit it! You see that, you chicken head? I hit it!"

"You call me chicken again, and I'm telling my mom," squealed David.

"O.K.," I snickered back reluctantly. "Now you throw yours."

Well, as time went on, those clings turned to clangs, and the pebbles turned to rocks. The louder the clang, the greater the accomplishment. Rocks turned to boulders, and then it happened.

I had the biggest boulder yet in the grasp of my hands. I sent it up with a mighty heave. Awkwardly, the huge boulder sailed over the fence, a twinge shot up my spine, and then, an unforgettable CRASH!

Fear shook my body. The twins next door were crying and shattered glass was all over the place.

"Right through the twins' window. Boy, are you going to get it!" squealed David.

At that instant, I heard my mom hollering my name. "Michael Gene, where are you?"

In an instant, my brilliant mind told me to hide. David and I dashed into the garage and bellyslid under the car. "I know you're in here," Mom squawked.

Soon, my fantastic hiding place was discovered, and David and I were in the hands of the authorities. The verdict was three weeks of being grounded and the incapability to sit down for a week.

Have you ever done something stupid like that?

My actions didn't please my parents or the neighbors (the twins either!), but you know what—they forgave me and still loved me.

It's time for a 3-point check:

Check #1. What does Ephesians 1:7 say about forgiveness? _____

_____

Check #2. Turn to I John 1:9 and put it into your own words.

_____

_____

Check #3. How far has God removed our sins from us
according to Psalm 103:12? _____

Do you need to ask the Lord to forgive you of
something today? Just bow your head and talk to Him about
it. Now make a conscious decision with your heart not to
return to that sin. Keep on growin'! I'll see you tomorrow!

Smiling because I am forgiven,

Mikey

*Asking for forgiveness can cleanse us from the dirt we
get into.*

★★ Day 33 ★★

Read Ephesians 1:15–23   check here _____

I love those old movies where some guy discovers
buried treasure. He follows his map to where ''X'' marks the
spot and then begins his digging. The digging continues until
someone's shovel makes a thudding noise against a solid
treasure chest. They raise the chest, shoot the lock off with
an old pistol, and raise the lid to see their treasure.

Today, let's picture these verses as a treasure map. We
are going digging for treasure. Get ready to dig, my friend!

Verses 15–16. Does Paul give thanks for these
people? What else does he do for them? _____

_____

_____

_____

Verses 17. What does Paul also pray that the Lord will give them? _____

_____

Verses 18–19. Now he prays that the eyes of their heart may be enlightened so that they can know 3 things.

1. _____

_____

2. _____

_____

3. _____

_____

In the last four verses (23–23), there are several statements about the Lord Jesus. Write down a few facts about Jesus.

1. _____

2. _____

3. _____

According to verse 22, who is in control? _____. That's right, Jesus. In Philippians 1:9–11, it says that someday every knee will bow and every tongue will confess that Jesus is Lord. What a day that will be! Good digging, buddy!

Don't forget to talk to the Lord today!

Discovering treasure with you,

Mikey

The Bible is the greatest treasure map leading us to the most precious treasure.

★★ **Day 34** ★★

Read Ephesians 2:1–3   check here _____

I don't know about you, but at times I have said, "If only Adam and Eve wouldn't have sinned, then everything would be okay around here." Have you ever pointed your finger at Adam and Eve?

Today's passage talks about sin. What does the word "sin" mean to you? _____

_____

_____

We sin when we fail to obey God or do things we know won't please Him. What does the last sentence in Ephesians 2:3 say? _____

_____

_____

Yes, by just being made the way we are, we naturally tend to do things that don't please God. Put in Adam and Eve's situation, we, too, would have eventually disobeyed God. We've got something inside us that doesn't want to please God. It is called sin.

Do you ever struggle when you do something you know you shouldn't do?

When an old Indian invited Christ into his life, he was asked to explain to his tribe what happened inside him. He explained it this way: "Two dogs are struggling and fighting to control me. One dog is white and the other is black."

"Which dog wins?" asked a warrior.

The wise old Indian replied, "Whichever dog I feed."

The struggle you experience in your Christian pilgrimage is normal. We all struggle at times. I know I do.

Let's be careful so sin doesn't control us, but we control sin!

Have a good day, my friend!

Struggling to win,

Mikey

No battle is won without a little struggle.   **67**

★★ **Day 35** ★★

Read Ephesians 2:4–7   check here _____

Yesterday's reading gave us a bit of bad news, but don't worry because today is full of good news. Fill in the good news below.

"But because of his great _____ for us, God, who is rich in _____, made us _____ even when we were dead in transgressions—it is by _____ you have been saved. And God raised us up with _____ and seated us with him in the _____ in Christ Jesus, in order that in the coming ages he might show the incomparable riches of his _____, expressed in his _____ to _____ in Christ Jesus."

Read it one more time after you fill in the blanks and put a check here _____. Wow! God loves us so much that He sent His Son to die for us. Our holy God can't tolerate sin, so he sent His Son to take care of our sin problem once and for all. YAHOOO!

Two brothers were playing in a sand yard one day when they fell into a shaft. The sand started to pour in around them as death stared them in the face.

"Get up on my shoulders," cried the oldest brother. "Maybe the sand won't cover you up."

The sand continued to fill the shaft. The younger brother stood on the shoulders of his brother as the sand covered the top of his head. He knew that his brother could not breathe. The sand continued to fall until the younger brother could no longer move his legs. As the sand began to cover the boy's shoulders his cry for help was finally heard.

A rescue team pulled him out and then went in for the older brother. They came out minutes later with a limp body.

The younger brother sat and cried and could be heard repeating these words: "He did it for me. He loved me and did it for me."

God sent a rescue team for us in the person of Jesus Christ. When was the last time you thanked Him for that? Take a minute and write a short thank-you note to God now.

Thankful for His love,

Mikey

Calvary is God's eternal heartache of love for you and me.

★★ **Day 36** ★★

Read Ephesians 2:8–10   **Check here** _____

A light snow fell as Jennifer sat looking out her window. The Christmas tree stood in the corner, glowing with delicate, sparkling lights. Presents rested under the tree. Joyful music was playing on the stereo, and everyone seemed to be a bit more cheerful—for tomorrow was Christmas.

Jennifer's family had just moved to New York from California. This big city of subways and high-rise buildings was a big change. But Jennifer's heart ached a bit because she was separated from her best friend, Christy. They had been best friends since kindergarten, and Christy's absence left a hollow feeling. Jennifer would try to have a nice Christmas, but it just wouldn't be the same.

While it was still dark the next morning, Jennifer's younger brother and sister began banging on everyone's door to wake them up. The excitement of opening presents was just ahead. Finally, all made their way to the family room. The young ones danced around the tree while Mom and Dad set up the video camera.

Before long, each member of the family sat with all his presents in front of him. After the family prayer, each member of the family opened a present. First, everyone opened the present that Jeff got them. Next, each opened the present from Mary. This went on until each of the children had one gift left—from Mom and Dad. The young ones knew this present was always the best, and the glow on their faces expressed it.

Jeff tore into the large box and found a new red bike like the one in the bike store window. Wait—this *was* the bike from the store window.

Mary neatly unwrapped her gift to find a complete Betty Crocker oven and kitchen set. She jumped up and down, screaming for joy, as she envisioned the meals she could help Mom out with, using her new oven.

Jennifer sat rolling her eyes, yet remembering a similar joy years ago. But she was older now, and almost ready to enter high school, so such excitement was "just for kids." Jennifer opened the box in front of her and found an envelope. Inside, she found two airline tickets for California. Her parents were going to let her spend the rest of the vacation back in California with Christy. Jennifer had a hard time holding in her excitement. She was overflowing with joy. But why did she have *two* airline tickets?

At that moment, in stepped a shadow from the kitchen. "Merry Christmas, Jennifer!"

It was Christy! Christy was in her house! Jennifer leaped over the boxes of opened presents and hugged her dear friend for what seemed like hours. They both cried with joy and soon sat on the couch, catching up on what had happened over the past few months. Before long, they would both be flying back to California to spend the rest of Christmas vacation together. It was the best Christmas ever.

Jennifer sure had some gracious parents, didn't she? Take a look at Ephesians 2:8 one more time with me. Write down the last six words of verse 8 below.

_____

God gave us salvation in the form of His Son, Jesus Christ. Nothing we could ever do would get us to heaven, so God provided the way for us by giving us His Son. We just need to receive His gift to us. Have you?

Have you thanked God for His gift to you today? Take a minute and do it right now.

Thankfully,

Mikey

The grace of God is nothing less than the unlimited love of God expressed in the gift of His Son, our Saviour.

★★ Day 37 ★★

Read Ephesians 2:11–18   check here _____

RESCUED

In the 1400s, a sailing vessel departed the local harbor in search for new lands. This discovery voyage was a dangerous one, and the crew knew it. They feared the unknown—coming against giant sea monsters and falling off the edge of the "flat" world.

They had been at sea for five weeks when a terrible storm began to toss them like a toy in a tub. The skies grew mysteriously dark and the winds were unpredictable. The crew knew what their job was—to keep this ship afloat and hang on for dear life! A storm at sea was the worst storm of all.

The storm pounded the small ship for two days. Several men had been swept overboard by the angry waves that covered the deck of the ship. Men began to lose hope as the storm continued its merciless downpour.

On the third day, the storm seemed to have gained even more momentum. The men had never seen such strong winds and high seas. Then, it happened.

The tiny ship could take the relentless pounding no more. The men tried to bail the water out, but it was coming in too fast. Once they heard the cracking of the wood, in just a matter of minutes the ship was sinking. The remaining crew held on to anything that would float and tied the flotation devices together. They all wondered if they would ever see the sun, or ever set their feet on solid ground again.

Time had passed, but the three survivors had no idea how much. They were still tied together and had been tossed upon the sandy beach of a small island. No life existed here, so they knew they would have to utilize their resources carefully, or they would soon starve.

Huts were built, and coconuts were collected. One of the men devised a fishing cage that provided a few fish each week. The daily diet of coconut milk, coconut meat, and fish got old real quick, but at least they were alive. Two of their shipmates' bodies had been washed ashore, and the men buried the bodies on the far side of the island. Deep inside, they wondered if they would ever see life again as they knew it.

One of the men kept track of how many days they had been stranded on the island by carving a line into a tree for each day. By this time, over three hundred lines covered the tree—almost one year.

Then one day as the sun was setting, there appeared the outlined figure of a ship far in the distance. It was pretty far off, but the men jumped up and down and waved huge coconut leaves. Slowly, the ship began to turn toward them. They were going to be rescued.

In what seemed like an eternity, the ship finally reached the island and anchored. They, too, were on a discovery mission from the country of Portugal. The survivors were to be on their way back home to see their loved ones once again.

Does Ephesians 2:13 say anything about us being stranded or far off from God? _____

_____

What in verse 13 brought us near again? _____

_____

_____

The rescue continues in verse 17. What does it say? ___

_____

_____

Who rescued us in verse 18? _____

Happily on shore with Jesus,

Mikey

We were all once shipwrecked and stranded on a lonely island until Jesus rescued us.

★★ Day 38 ★★

Read Ephesians 2:19–22   **check here** _____

Years ago, a large square stone was placed at the corner of where a building was to be built. All the other stones would be placed according to this major stone. This stone was called the cornerstone and the most important stone of the entire building.

In today's passage, Jesus is called the cornerstone. All of us "bricks" are built upon Him. He is our foundation. Try to find all the construction words in Ephesians 2:19–22 and then try to locate them in the puzzle on the next page.   73

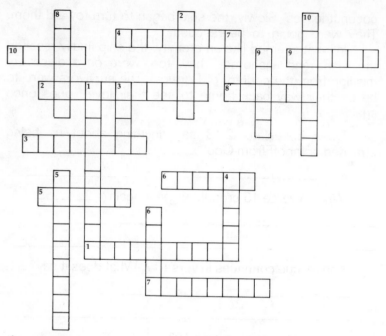

Across

1. We are no longer _____ and aliens.
2. The type of stone that Jesus is.
3. We are being built in this way to become a dwelling in which God lives.
4. Another word for what a home is.
5. The 43rd word beginning with "consequently" in v. 19.
6. The whole building becomes a holy _____ in the Lord.
7. Kids play with these kind of blocks.
8. Last word in v. 22.
9. My last name.
10. Best book in the world.

Down

1. You've got to have a solid _____ or you may be building on sinking sand. *(Spell it backwards!)*
2. Another word for an out-of-space visitor—more than one.
3. Jesus said He would do this from the dead.

74

4. Jesus _____ (rhymes with gives).
5. We are members of God's _____.
6. 1st word of v. 20. *(Spell this one backwards, too.)*
7. "_____ people, _____ household."
8. "But _____ citizens with God's people."
9. Jesus is the _____ cornerstone.
10. "_____ and prophets."

Good job, my friend! I'll talk to you tomorrow. Don't forget me!

Never puzzled with Jesus,

Mikey

The cornerstone that was rejected became the cornerstone of a whole new world.

★★ Day 39 ★★

Read Ephesians 3:1–6   **check here** _____

The summer of 1978 was special for me. In fact, it changed my life. I was selected to be a member of a basketball team that would tour the Philippines. Before and after each game we would talk with the people. At half-time we sang a few songs and then shared how Jesus had come into our lives.

It was the fourth night of our tour. My body was gleaming from sweat after playing in the first half, and I was standing at half-court with a microphone in my hand. I began to share about Jesus and how He was Lord of my life. After the game we were flooded with people asking questions and signing up for a Bible study. More importantly, over thirty came to receive Jesus Christ into their lives that night.

The Lord taught me a lesson that night in a gym located in the jungle area of Mindinao. He taught me that the message of Jesus was for all people regardless of the color of their skin, the language they spoke, or how they dressed. Those I spoke to were different than I was but they were still beautiful people who needed to hear about the Lord.

Playing basketball all summer was fun. We went 40–0 and grew really close as a team. Yet, the best part of the trip was seeing people respond to Jesus Christ.

Can you think of three people who haven't asked Jesus into their life yet? Write down their names below.

1. _____

2. _____

3. _____

Now let's take one more step. Pray for them and their need for Jesus. I hope you get a chance to talk to them soon. You are special, my friend!

Because the world needs to know,

Mikey

The message of Christ is a message for every man, woman, and child on the face of the earth.

★★ Day 40 ★★

Read Ephesians 3:7–13   check here _____

They had been digging for hours and still had found nothing. The captain studied the treasure map again to see if they were in the right place. As far as he could tell, they were digging right where the "X" was located.

Finally, the captain heard his men yell. They had hit a hard object. The men dug with a new spark of energy. It was just what they were searching for—the treasure chest of the Armadillo. After a few hours the chest sat upon the sand. The

captain spoke to his crew.

"You know why you were chosen to come on this mission. You are the best men in all the land. Each one of you will be paid more than you can imagine for your efforts. There will be enough to share among the poor of our homeland, and that is what we will do. In this way our riches will touch many instead of just a few."

The men all stood proudly around the chest. A shot rang out as the padlock slid off its once-tight hold. The clasps were unfastened and the lid was slowly raised. The entire crew stood speechless. In front of them sat a chest full of jewels, gold coins, pearls, and precious stones—more riches than any man could ever spend.

What verse talks about the "unsearchable riches of Christ?" _____

_____

If someone asked you, "What is so great about being a Christian?" what would you answer? _____

_____

These are real riches. Sure, gold could make you happy for a while but what about after a while? All the jewels in the world can't buy eternal life! We have found a treasure *more* valuable than silver or gold.

Rich in Christ,

Mikey

The riches of man don't compare to the riches of Christ.

★★ Day 41 ★★

Read Ephesians 3:14–19   **check here** _____

Hello, my friend. I am proud of you and your progress in this book. Keep up the great work, and don't forget to mark your progress on the calendar.

Do you know what happens if a person stops breathing? If not corrected, it's all over for that person.

Prayer is like breathing because it's real important to   77 keep our relationship with the Lord alive. Someone gave me this letter, and I want to share it with you:

Dear Friend,

How are you? I just had to send a note to tell you how much I love you and care about you.

I saw you yesterday as you were walking with your friends. I waited all day hoping you would want to talk with me also. As evening drew near, I gave you a sunset to close your day and a cool breeze to rest you—I waited. You never came. Yes, it did hurt me, but I still love you because I am your friend.

I saw you fall asleep last night and longed to touch your brow, so I spilled moonlight upon your pillow and face. Again I waited, wanting to rush down so we could talk. I have so many gifts for you! You awakened late and rushed off to work. My tears were in the rain.

Today you look so sad—so all alone. It makes my heart ache because I understand. My friends let me down and hurt me so many times, too, but I love you.

Oh! If only you would listen to me. *I love you!* I try to tell you in the blue sky and in the quiet green grass. I whisper it in the rustling leaves and breathe it into the colorful flowers. I shout it to you in the mountain streams and give the birds love songs to sing. I clothe you with warm sunshine and perfume the air with nature scents. My love for you is deeper than the oceans and bigger than the biggest want or need in your heart. Oh! If you only knew how much I want to help you. I want you to meet my father. He wants to help you, too. My father is like that, you know.

Just call me—ask me—talk with me. Please, please, don't forget me. I have so much to share with you.

Okay, I won't hassle you any further. You are free to choose me. It is your decision. I have chosen you; I will wait because I LOVE YOU.

Your Friend,
Jesus Christ

Now look up these three verses and write a comment about what these say about prayer.

Ephesians 3:16 _____

John 15:17 _____

I Peter 5:6–7 _____

I'll talk to you tomorrow. Don't forget to talk to God today.

In prayer for you,

Mikey

Prayer allows us to keep in touch with Him who loves us most.

★★ **Day 42** ★★

Read Ephesians 3:20–21   **check here** _____

In my life I have prayed for some pretty big things, and it has been exciting to see God answer those prayers through the years. He is bigger than my biggest prayer need, and He wants to hear from me because He cares about me.

Here are a few big prayers of mine and how they were answered.

- I prayed to play ball for Him overseas.
- *He allowed me to be picked in 1978 to go to the Philippines.*
- I prayed that the Lord might give me a wife.
- *Leesa and I were married on July 24, 1982.*
- I prayed for a job in a solid church.
- *June 1, 1984, the Lord led me to a great church.* **79**

- I prayed with my wife for a baby.
- *Sept. 2, 1985, the Lord gave us a son, Michael.*
- *June 2, 1987, the Lord gave us a daughter, Katie.*

I could go on and on. Do you have big dreams like these? Have you prayed about them? God isn't a "request line" but He does want to meet the needs of His children.

Here's a fun project to do that I've done several times. In the space below, write a letter to God as you would write a friend. Share your dreams and concerns. You'll feel great!

Dear heavenly Father,

_____

_____

_____

_____

_____

Because He is able,

Mikey

Our Father is able to meet our needs if we just take time to ask.

★★ **Day 43** ★★

Read Ephesians 4:1–3   check here _____

They had just finished ten of the toughest weeks of their lives. These past ten weeks made boot camp look like a girls' slumber party. Out of the thirty men in this regiment, only three would be chosen to bear the name of the Green Berets. To be a Green Beret was one of the highest compliments a soldier could receive. You were the top of your class in hand-to-hand combat, survival tactics, and demolition expertise.

When a soldier made the ranking of Green Beret, he was given a special uniform and expected to walk in a manner worthy of that uniform on and off the base. You know, we don't wear a special uniform, but if you have asked Jesus into your life, you do have a special name—Christian. To be a Christian means that you are a follower of Jesus Christ, a Christ one. Just as the soldier is expected to walk in a manner worthy of his uniform, so we, too, are expected to walk in a manner worthy of our name.

In verses 2 and 3, Paul gives us several practical ways to live a life worthy of the Lord. Can you list them?

Be _____ and _____.

_____ in love.

Keep _____.

Now circle one and commit yourself to working on it. I know which one I am going to work on today.

Thanks for meeting with me again. You are special to me, my friend!

Seeking to keep His name clean,

Mikey

To bear the name Christian is to state your allegiance to the greatest army of all.

★★ Day 44 ★★

Read Ephesians 4:4–10   check here _____

ONE WAY

Some people have a hard time accepting the truth of our Christian faith. They call us narrow-minded and ''tight in our thinking.''

"How could there be just one way to heaven?" they ask.

If I were very ill and the doctors had a known cure, I would begin treatment right away. I would want whatever medicine the doctor prescribed for me and expect it to work as it had for others. It wouldn't help me to argue that my doctor was narrow-minded because he just had one type of medicine to cure my illness.

Now put God in the doctor's place. He has given us the "medicine" we need for our sin problem in the person of Jesus Christ. The blood He shed on the cross was the price needed for us to have our sins forgiven. You may know others who call that narrow-minded, but that doesn't change the way God has provided salvation to man.

Look at these passages and write what they mean in your own words.

Acts 4:12 _____

Matthew 7:13—14 _____

John 14:6 _____

Now look at Ephesians 4:4—6. Write down the words that come after the word "one."

one _____

one _____

one _____

one _____

one _____ one _____ one _____ & one _____

Christianity isn't narrow-minded. It just states the way our heavenly Father lovingly reached down to mankind to provide salvation. We don't have to do anything but accept His gift. Have you accepted His gift?

One way to heaven,

Mikey

82   *Christianity is the story of God reaching down to man.*

★★ Day 45 ★★

Read Ephesians 4:11–16   check here _____

What verse today talks about growing up in Christ? We do need to grow up, don't we? I mean if I came to your house and you were still in diapers, I'd be shocked (and leave pretty quick, too!).

A child's mind is different than ours. Let's take a six-year-old as an example. A six-year-old is curious and adventurous. He asks questions such as how high heaven is, if the moon is really of cheese, and what God looks like. Here is a little story of a six-year-old boy. Imagine the mind of this little fellow and get ready to giggle a little.

THROUGH A CHILD'S EYES

Spring is sprung
the grass is riz
I wonder where the flowers is?

The rain stopped last week so now I could go out and play. Mom said that it was spring now, and we could go outside and plant flowers again. I didn't like to plant flowers. You see, I always felt sorry for the flowers. Once, when I was little (I'm six now!) I cried. I cried because when the rain stops and the sun comes out my mom plants pretty flowers. Then, whenever she wants to, she'll go out and cut them half off— right above the belly button!

I don't understand.

It must have hurt the poor flowers to be planted, loved, cared for, and then killed by the same person who made them. I know if my mom tried to cut me off at the belly button, I'd run! The flowers   83 would run, too, but you see, their feet grow under the ground.

I don't understand that either.

Outside the sky is a pretty blue and the sun warms my face. I like that. Then, the door slams and out steps the butcher. My lip starts to tremble so I bite it so I won't cry. Calmly, she kneels down. The sky darkens as her shadow peers over the defenseless flowers. The scissors sparkle in the sunlight as they are placed right above the belly button. Then, SNIP! The stem weakens and the flower slowly falls, like when I put too many blocks on top of each other. It falls and lies dead on the ground.

I walk briskly past my mom and hear her singing these words,

> "Don't you know
> That flowers grow
> To give themselves away?"

I was really upset now. I was so upset that I ran in the house and stubbed my big toe on the doorstep (I almost said a bad word, too!). Those flowers didn't want to die. They weren't even old yet. The least she could have done was let the flowers grow old, and then kill them. She took the flowers into the house and put them into a nice vase. Then she left the room.

The flowers sat there on the table. They looked alive still, but I knew they were dead, and when you're dead, you're dead for good. I knew 'cause my frog died in my pocket last Thursday. I prayed he'd be alive again but it didn't happen. He just stayed all smushed up. Why did the flowers have to die?

I just don't understand.

At Sunday school today I learned about a man. He was just like the flowers. I mean he wasn't a flower but he was kind of the same. You see, this man lived his whole life to give it away just like the flowers did. His whole life was spent giving, loving, and caring for other people. And you know what? He was killed by those same people when he was still young. This man could have gotten away if he wanted to, but he had it all planned out. He gave himself away so that all

men could see God again. This man was more than a vase or

a table decoration. He was God and his name was Jesus.

I guess we'll plant some more flowers again sometime, but that's O.K., because . . . *now* I understand.

> *Don't you know*
> *That flowers grow*
> *To give themselves away?*
>
> *Truly I say to you,*
> *Unless you are converted*
> *And become like children*
> *You shall not enter the*
> *Kingdom of Heaven.*
> Matt. 18:3

Make it a point to share a smile with someone today. When you see a child, remember this little story.

You are more special than you know,

Mikey

To grow up in Christ, we have to stretch a little.

★★ Day 46 ★★

Read Ephesians 4:17–24   check here _____

A few years ago a telephone company made some major bucks on a particular commercial. The commercial message was, "Reach out, reach out, and touch someone— reach out, reach out, and just say hi."

Do you remember hearing that commercial on television? Some of the most sentimental commercials involve a hug or someone's touch. We are sensitive to a mother hugging a son who has been away in the army or a little girl cuddling up to her daddy. Think for a minute and see if you can come up with three commercials that have someone hugging or touching someone else. You know, the kind that give you warm fuzzies all over.

1. _____

2. _____

3. _____ 85

It's amazing how many times Jesus touched someone. He touched children, blind eyes, those who needed support of some kind, and even those who were labeled "untouchable" because of leprosy.

Verse 23 in today's reading says, "To be made new _____."

Verse 24 adds, "and to put on _____, created to be like _____."

If Jesus wasn't afraid to give a hug or lend His touch to those who were hurting, then neither should we. Can you think of someone's life you could warm up today by a pat on the back or a gentle hug? How about your mom or dad? What about that best friend of yours? Share a part of yourself today.

Sharing lots of hugs,

Mikey

A hug is a special gift from you to another that comes from the heart.

★★ Day 47 ★★

Read Ephesians 4:25–28   check here _____

"Anger is God's alarm system to let me know that there is some right I have not yielded over to Him or some right that I have tried to take away from Him." Someone once told that to me when I was in high school, and almost ten years later it is still fresh in my mind.

Let's face it, we all get angry. But how do we respond to others and even ourselves when we get angry? That's what matters. Angry feelings that are held inside can make us critical of others and bring out the worst in us. Put simply, suppressed anger puts you in one rotten mood!

Being honest with others, talking things over, and dealing with our anger is the right way to handle anger. My wife and I made an agreement when we were first married. The agreement was that we would not go to sleep angry at each other. Since then we have had a few late night talks, but we go to sleep with good feelings instead of a bitter taste in our mouths.

When was the last time you got angry? Write down what happened. _____

_____

Now, what was your attitude of anger like? Were you so mad you swore? Were you so mad that you said, "I hate you?" Were you just upset about a situation and can deal with it now? Jot down your attitude. _____

_____

What do verses 26–27 say specifically about anger and your life? _____

_____

We all get angry at times, but God wants us to be careful not to sin in our anger. Now that's hard. Start making progress today, my friend. I'll meet with you again tomorrow. "Same bat time, same bat station." (Remember that show?)

Putting God first,

Mikey

When a person's temper gets the best of him, it often reveals the worst of him.

★★ Day 48 ★★

Read Ephesians 4:29–32   **check here** _____

Can you think of some good and bad uses of fire? A fire is your best friend after you have been out in real cold weather. Have you ever had your hand or toes hurt because of the cold? But what a relief when you can kick those boots off and toss those gloves aside and begin to feel warmth in those limbs again. A big roaring fire seems to bring life back into your hands and feet.

A fire can be your worst enemy, though. I remember hearing the screaming of sirens one night for what seemed like hours. The next day as I was walking to school with my friend we saw the charcoal remains of a once beautiful two-story house.

The words that come out of our mouths are kind of like fire. They can be words that warm others up and bring comfort, or they can be words that destroy and burn others up. What kind of words will come out of your mouth today?

How should we talk according to verse 29? (It's a great verse to memorize.) _____
_____

What are the words we need to get rid of in verse 31?

_____ _____ _____

_____ _____ _____

What is our language supposed to be like? Look at verse 32.

What comes out of our mouths *does* have an impact on others. I am sure you have had a day ruined by what someone said about you or to you. Those fiery darts hurt! Check out this poem.

POWER OF WORDS

A careless word may kindle strife.
A cruel word may wreck a life.
A bitter word may hate instill;
A brutal word may smite and kill.

A gracious word may smooth the way.
A joyous word may light the day.
A timely word may lessen stress;
A loving word may heal and bless.
                                    Author unknown

Building up others with my mouth,

Mikey

Our mouths are to help build others up, not tear them down.

★★ Day 49 ★★

Read Ephesians 5:1–2   check here _____

He was just three years old, and he loved to imitate his father. When dad pulled out the lawn mower and began mowing the lawn, a little figure followed a few feet behind him pushing his own lawn mower. It was quite a sight to see Dad followed by his son whose little lawn mower spurted out bubbles.

A little later Dad began to wash the car. Soap covered the car, and down by the hub caps sat a little figure copying his father's scrubbing motion. Those hub caps had never been so clean!

The day continued on with son just a few steps behind Dad, imitating whatever he did. The washing of the car was followed by raking leaves, emptying the garbage, cutting wood, and painting the fence.

After dinner, Dad sat down in his chair to relax after a good day's work. He rested with the thought that he had finished several projects in just one Saturday. He then glanced down and noticed his son resting in the same position that he was in. He had been by his father's side all day, and the little guy was tuckered out.

"Did you have a good day today, son?" asked Dad in a relaxed voice.

The little boy looked up with a big smile and said, "I had a good day helping you, Dad. When I grow up, I want to be just like you. You are the best dad in the whole wide world." **89**

With that, the boy jumped into his father's lap, and Dad enjoyed a big bear hug. He loved his son and was proud to have him imitate him.

The love that this three-year-old little boy had for his father caused him to imitate him. True love does that. It causes us to conform and be like the one we love.

What do the first four words of chapter 5 say? _____

_____

What does it mean to imitate someone? _____

_____

Yes, God wants us to imitate Him. That means we need to be open and honest with our heavenly Father. We do love God and we do want to be like Him. Where do we find out what God is like?

That's right, the Bible. As we read about Jesus we can see how God wants us to live. We can imitate God!

Write down three things you would like to imitate in your relationship with God today.

1. _____

2. _____

3. _____

Keep up the great work, my friend. You are doing super! I care about you!

Imitating my heavenly Dad,

Mikey

True love causes us to imitate the one we love.

★★ Day 50 ★★

Read Ephesians 5:3–10   check here _____

Alexander the Great conquered almost all of the known world in the last half of the fourth century before Christ. To be a part of his great army was one of the highest honors a man could receive. In fact, it has been said that men would celebrate for days if a son was born to him, realizing that this son might become part of this great army. It has also been said that such sorrow was felt in the birth of a daughter that a father might take that child's life.

The ranks of Alexander's army held their heads high, knowing they were the most powerful army in all the world. In this army, to run away from the line of battle meant you were a disgrace and would soon face death.

One particular battle was a tough one. For hours the clashing of metal and struggle of man against man could be heard. A young soldier was near the front and fear crept into him as he saw a man cry out as a sword pierced through his chest. He turned the other way and saw more of the same. Tired and scared, the young lad threw down his sword and ran for safety.

Alexander's army emerged the victor, and the young boy was brought before the greatest soldier of all, Alexander the Great. He sheepishly moved forward before the court, yet remained several feet away from the throne where Alexander sat.

Alexander began to speak in his rich, deep voice directly to the boy.

"Young man, you know what you have done, and you are aware of the penalty of your actions. Do you have anything to say for yourself?"

The boy simply stood staring at the ground as he shook his head.

"Son, I must ask you one question. What is your name?"

The boy began to squirm some and replied in a whisper, "Alexander."

This caught the great commander by surprise, and he quickly thought of a lesson that no man would ever forget.

"Look me in the eyes, soldier, and tell me your name!" Alexander's voice sounded more like thunder this time.

The boy looked up and said, "My father named me after you, sir, and my name is Alexander."

The crowd was so silent you could have heard a pin drop. They wondered if the commander would unleash his sword on the youth or allow the executioner to exercise his **91** muscles. Everyone sat in awe, waiting to see what would happen next.

"I'm going to ask you one more time, young man, now what is your name?" Now Alexander's voice roared, and he was even pointing at the young boy.

"My name, sir, is Alexander."

The commander rose up off his seat and proceeded down the steps one at a time toward the young man. The crowd was in a tense fever looking to see if his hand was on his sword. He came before the lad and firmly gripped his shoulders. Then he spoke these words that would never be erased from the crowd's memory.

"Son," Alexander the Great said in a strong voice so everyone could hear, *"you either change your name, or change your ways."*

With that, the young man was set free, determined more than ever to live up to his name.

We have a name, too. It is Christian. My question to you is this: how do you wear it? Are you able to hold your head high or do you sheepishly look to the ground in shame? Would Jesus Christ be proud of the way you bear His name or ashamed? Are you a real soldier or more of a cub scout? Take a minute and make a conscious decision to live up to your name!

In verses 3 and 4, what are the things we as Christians need to be sure are not among us? _____

_____

Who doesn't have a heavenly inheritance according to verse 5? _____

_____

Now write verse 8 and verse 10 in your own words. ____

_____

Have a great day and wear your name with pride.

Proud of my name—Christian,

Mikey

My name tells others who I am following.

P.S. Congratulations on completing 50 days! I really am proud of you!

★★ **Day 51** ★★

Read Ephesians 5:11–14   check here _____

EXPOSED BY THE LIGHT

They were to meet at 2:00 A.M. in the dark alley behind the liquor store. If the deal was successful, it would be the largest drug deal ever made in the city. It was a cold, gloomy night, and the thought of buying the drugs sent chills up the spine. Indeed, it would be a night these two would never forget.

At 1:00 A.M. the two buyers left the house with two suitcases packed with money. It took two suitcases because the seller wanted small bills so the money would not be traced.

They sat in the dark alley for almost an hour before a car pulled into the alley. The dealer stepped out of the car and made his way toward the two men with the suitcases. A few words were exchanged and both parties appeared pleased. The money was checked over, as were the drugs, by each side. The deal was ready to be made.

The two men sat the suitcases full of money to one side. The dealer then sat his suitcase to the other side. As each went to grab the other's suitcase, a tremendous bright light blinded the men from straight above them. Two more lights came on an instant later from each side of the alley.

"Stop where you are and put your hands behind your   **93** head," ordered a policeman from behind the dumpster. The biggest drug deal in the city had just become the largest drug bust in the state. All of those involved were apprehended and sent to prison for their crimes.

Now read this passage again (5:11–14), and mark here when you have read it _____. Did you really read it? Now come on, you read it.

These guys were participating in the unfruitful deeds of darkness. Their deeds became visible under the bright police lights.

Did you know that your every move is seen by God? He cares about you and wants you to do what is pleasing to Him. Let's put those little deeds of darkness aside and live for the Lord!

Open before God,

Mikey

All things become visible when they are exposed by the light.

★★ Day 52 ★★

Read Ephesians 5:15–17   check here _____

I don't think there is a pain that hurts more than when you lose a loved one. When someone who was close to you is there no longer, there seems to be an empty spot in your life. You know that life must go on but you hurt because you know it must now go on without that special person.

My grandma was a special person in my life. She was a godly woman who loved us grandkids beyond words. She rode a motorcycle 'til she was nearly fifty and always had a song in her heart. She even sang while cleaning the house! Visiting grandma always was a joy for me, and I will treasure the moments we shared forever. Her gray hair and warm smile made her the most attractive grandma in the world. She always had a kind word to say, and she always found some way to help others out. You can probably tell that my Grandma and I had a very special relationship.

I'll never forget the pain in my heart when the call came

that told me that grandma was with the Lord. Cancer finally took her life. I jumped on a plane and flew home for the funeral. The aching of my heart was just too much to bear. I remember going off to be by myself and talk to the Lord alone. I just had to tell the Lord how much I missed her and how much I loved her. I don't think I've ever cried so hard in all my life. Just writing about it gets me all choked up again. Praise God I will see her again someday.

One thing really stands out in my mind about Grandma. Not only was she a godly woman, but she used her time here on earth wisely. I can't remember her wasting half the day in front of the T.V. I do remember her sharing her life with others and living her life for God.

If you knew you were going to die next week, I bet from now until then you wouldn't scream at your parents, argue with your brothers and sisters, or sit in front of the "boob tube" for hours. You would probably change a few things, wouldn't you? What would you change?

1. _____

2. _____

Good, my friend. Now write Ephesians 5:15−17 in your own words. _____

_____

_____

Making the most of my time,

Mikey

Live as God wants you to—time is running out.

★★ Day 53 ★★

Read Ephesians 5:18–21   **check here** _____

MUSIC THAT MINISTERS

One of the main factors that helped me grow as a young Christian was Christian music. My music ability doesn't go far beyond the ability of being able to push the power button on my stereo, but I still love music.

The right kind of music can really allow me to make melody with my heart to the Lord. Christian music can help me focus my thoughts on the Lord, and at times it can even help me express my love for Him in words that don't come easily for me. I think it is great to be able to sing along with a song that has Scripture in it or to think about the Lord while I sing a song to Him. These are growing times for me, and I hope you have some good Christian music of your own.

Music, like many things in life, can be used to our benefit or to our detriment. Some music can hurt us and our relationship with God. Some music can help us grow in our relationship with God.

What kind of music do you listen to most of the time? Do you have any Christian music that you like? When was the last time you spent a few dollars at a Christian bookstore for a record? With artists like Amy Grant, Michael W. Smith, Leon Patillo, Russ Taff, David Meece, and Bryan Duncan, there is no excuse. Give Christian music a fair chance in your life.

Singing for Jesus,

Mikey

Are you listening to music that is a burden or music that lightens the load?

★★ Day 54 ★★

Read Ephesians 5:22–33   check here _____

Today's passage is about husbands and wives. This special chapter in life is still ahead of you. So today, I'd like to share something very personal and very special that I wrote for my wife. It's a little fairy tale dedicated to the young lady who has made the land of hopes and dreams a place of reality for me. I pray that you will someday have a partner as special as Leesa is to me.

Once upon a time, in the Land of Hopes and Dreams, all the frogs dreamed of living in the Frogville garden of the beautiful Princess Leesa. There was a beautiful pond filled with plush green lily pads and flowers. Bite-size flies roamed the skies making any meal delicious.

One day, as Webbfeet High School dismissed their classes, all the frogs could tell something strange was about to happen. The sky was a murky gray, and a light misty fog was slowly seeping over the trees. Frogs stopped croaking and bugs stopped buzzing while they waited for something to happen.

Then through a sudden flash of lightning, a roar of thunder, and a hazy layer of smoke, a figure could be seen in the distance—the Wicked Wizard.

Every living frog feared the Wizard. He stood as tall as a willow tree, wore a long black robe, and had a mean wrinkled face and long sharp fingernails. The frightened frogs began to hop away when he spoke.

"Stop where you are, you slimey green creatures," ordered the Wizard in a strong, firm voice. "I come to warn you. You have until the next full moon to pack your things and leave Princess Leesa's garden. For I, the Wizard, am going to destroy Frogville and capture the beautiful Princess Leesa and her kingdom." Then the Wizard lifted his cape over his eyes and disappeared in a mystified puff of smoke.

All the frogs began to worry. The next full moon was only three days away. The frog-elders called an emergency meeting, then the head elder slowly and regretfully announced that every frog should pack and be ready to leave in three days. Mothers, fathers, polliwogs, and even toads wept in grief for their pads, their land, but mostly for Princess Leesa.

You see, Princess Leesa was the nicest, sweetest, most beautiful human being in the world to the little green frogs. She considered all of the little creatures her very own **97** special "little green friends." One special little frog, Mikey, was very troubled. Mikey could remember his old grandpa toad telling him about the special Green Cave, where there was the magic Golden Sword to kill the Wicked Wizard. So Mikey went in search of the Green Cave.

At sunset the first day, Mikey reached the foot of the Wizard's Mountain. He was tired and scared but there wasn't time to rest, so the little frog began to climb up, and up, and up. The thought of his home pad, his friends, and mostly the beautiful Princess Leesa kept him climbing.

The second day's climb was much the same. The rocks were getting steeper and the trails harder. Mikey continued to climb until all of a sudden he was peering into the eyes of the biggest frog-eating snake he had ever seen.

"I want you," hissed the snake in a raspy voice as he slithered closer to the little frog.

The little frog gulped in fear. "I-I-I must get to the Green Cave quickly. Please let me pass, or maybe you could take me there."

"I will take you there my little friend. I will take you there once you are in my stomach!" shouted the evil snake.

As Mikey's red eyes saw those sharp white fangs dash at him, he jumped. The snake barely missed the little frog and fell off the cliff to a long death. That second night was a tiring one as Mikey fought sleep. The third day seemed to last forever, but in the distance he saw a glittering light.

As he pulled his body over the top of the next crest, he

was blinded by a bright light. Slowly the little frog opened each eye and saw the glowing Green Cave.

"I have made it, Grandpa Toad," whispered the little frog in a tired breath.

Ever so slowly, Mikey carefully stepped into the Green Cave. He gradually looked around the cave until he found the Golden Sword, mounted in a huge rock and glowing a shiny, brilliant gold. On the rock was an engraving.

IN THIS SWORD RESIDES THE POWER TO DEFEAT THE WIZARD. TO THE ONE WHO TOUCHES AND REMOVES THIS SWORD WILL THE POWER BE-LONG.

Mikey cautiously approached the sword. With all the concentration he had, Mikey began to slowly ease the Golden Sword out of the rock. Its power gripped the little frog, and he smiled with amazement.

Meanwhile, the frogs from Frogville tearfully stood on a nearby hill to face the destruction of their land. With an exploding flash of lightning, the Wicked Wizard appeared beside the town of Frogville.

"Aha!" shouted the Wicked Wizard. "Now I will destroy your land and capture the beautiful Princess Leesa."

As the Wizard started to raise his arms to destroy the land, a golden flame shot through the air followed by a cloud of smoke. There, in front of the Wizard, stood Mikey with the Golden Sword.

"I promised to destroy any slimey green creatures that remained, and it looks like you're the first," mocked the Wizard in a deep voice.

Mikey stood firm with the Golden Sword and warned the Wicked Wizard, "I will kill you with this Golden Sword."

"Nothing can stop me from destroying this land and taking Princess Leesa for myself." the Wizard shouted angrily.

The Wizard began throwing magical balls of fire at Mikey. Carefully, he shifted the Golden Sword in a position to reflect the next ball of fire right back to the Wizard.

"My eyes! I can't see!" screamed the Wizard in blinding pain.

Then Mikey took careful aim at the Wizard's heart. The

Wizard gasped for breath and began melting until all that was left was his old black robe.

The crowd cheered with excitement as they hopped back to congratulate Mikey. But the closer they hopped, the quieter they became. Soon all could see little Mikey lying unconscious. They carried Mikey to a special bed, made of several thick green lily pads and surrounded by beautiful flowers. The whole population of Frogville waited for the first movements of Mikey.

By morning there was still no change in Mikey. Finally, the elders called an emergency meeting and then announced that five frogs would be needed to go see Princess Leesa and bring her to Mikey. The quiet afternoon passed slowly, but at sunset, a voice could be heard in the distance.

"They're coming! Princess Leesa is coming!"

Princess Leesa spoke softly, "Show me where Mikey is. He saved my land, my friends, and my life."

Every head turned to Mikey. The princess gracefully moved over to Mikey and knelt beside him. "Thank you, Mikey," she said in a quivering voice. Then she kissed the little frog, and there, right next to the princess, stood the handsomest prince in all the land. Prince Mike and Princess Leesa lived happily ever after.

From one frog to another,

Mikey

Husband and wives give a lifetime of giving to each other.

★★ Day 55 ★★

Read Ephesians 6:1–4   check here _____

I was just a little squirt of three or four. One hot summer day, my dad began barbecuing the chicken for dinner.

"Now don't ride your tricycle around this barbecue, Michael," my dad warned.

I responded kindly, letting Dad know I understood his words.

100   Well, time went by and I was getting bored. I mean how

long does it take to barbecue a stupid chicken? My mind began to figure out a course I could take on my tricycle without hitting the barbecue. There would be only one dangerous turn by the old chicken, and I was sure I could make it just fine.

Eagerly, I jumped on my red and white tricycle and began peddling as fast as I could on the backyard course. I flew past the sandbox. The tricycle was breaking some major speed records when I came onto the covered patio and prepared myself for the dangerous turn ahead. My fat little legs were peddling as fast as they could by the barbecue, and it seemed like I had made it safely. Then, it happened.

Just as a big smile broke across my face, I felt a tremendous tug from the back of my bike. The cord from the barbeque had gotten caught in my back tire, and now the whole barbecue was falling toward the pavement.

Crash! The barbecue smashed against the ground, red hot briquets spilled all over the patio, and the chicken was spinning around on the ground at full speed. I guess it was trying to run away, too, because here came my dad! Oh no!

When Dad came out the door, he looked like the Jolly Green Giant. His chicken was still spinning at full speed, and by now the cat was making sport of the live meal on the ground. Dad unplugged the barbecue, and the chicken surrendered.

"I didn't do it, the tricycle did it, the tricycle did it," I began to yell at the top of my lungs.

My dad did something strange. He didn't spank me (at least not yet) but picked me up and hugged me real tight.

Why do you think my dad hugged me at the sight of the overturned barbecue and all the hot coals? _____

_____

Why do you think my dad warned me in the first place? Was it because he didn't want me to have any fun? _____

_____

What could I have missed if I just would have obeyed my dad? (Clue—it had to do with the seat of my pants! Ouch!)

_____

_____

What is the action and the attitude we should have toward our parents in Ephesians 6:1–2?

Action _____

Attitude _____

Will you try and remember this story next time your parents ask you to do or not to do something? They often have good reasons!

Obeying & honoring with you,

Mikey

If we obey our parents, we will miss a lot of pain and trouble.

★★ Day 56 ★★

Read Ephesians 6:5–9   check here _____

Over forty years ago, our nation faced one of its most disastrous days. Early in the morning of December 7, 1941, while negotiations between American and Japanese diplomats were taking place to bring about peace, the Japanese launched an all-out attack on the U.S. naval base at Pearl Harbor. Flying through the night, over one hundred airplanes and numerous submarines carried out the destruction at Pearl Harbor. Eight American battleships and ten other naval vessels were sunk or badly damaged, nearly two hundred American aircraft were destroyed, and approximately three thousand naval and military personnel were killed or wounded. This attack marked Japan's entrance into World War II on the side of Germany and Italy, and prompted the United States to declare war on these three countries and soon enter World War II.

It's easy to take America for granted. Although we haven't been in the midst of war, we need to remember that we have our freedom because men were willing to give up their lives. Maybe your father or grandfather remembers living through a time of war. Why don't you ask them? We can be thankful that we haven't had to face war and that we live in a free country, where we are allowed to worship as we please. Write a short prayer thanking God for the freedom we have.

Thankful for my freedom,

Mikey

America, God has shed His grace on thee!

★★ Day 57 ★★

Read Ephesians 6:10–24   **check here** _____

A Roman soldier was always ready for battle, always prepared for the struggle ahead. He was a man of war—a fighting machine, quick to conquer when given the chance.

Can you picture Paul, as he writes this letter, being distracted by a Roman soldier on patrol duty? Then, toying with the idea in his mind, he begins to take each piece of the soldier's armor and transfer it to the Christian. Fully equiped, the Christian soldier, too, can have victory in each daily battle.

Let's look at our battle a little closer.

Who is our battle against? We have to know who we are fighting! (v. 12) _____

Why should we put on the full armor of God? (v. 13) ___

_____

What are the pieces of armor?

103

belt _____

breastplate _____

feet _____

shield _____

helmet _____

sword _____

Now find the explanation on the right that matches up with the armor on the left for the Christian soldier.

_____ Belt of truth	A. The Word of God—your Bible.
_____ Breastplate of righteousness	B. Can extinguish all the flaming arrows of the evil one.
_____ Feet fitted with the readiness that comes from the gospel of peace.	C. A Christian soldier speaks the truth in love.
_____ Shield of faith	D. A Christian soldier is committed to a life of right living—true character that is vital.
_____ Helmet of salvation	E. A Christian soldier is ready to share the gospel wherever his feet lead him.
_____ Sword of the spirit	F. The message of the Christian soldier is life that opens eyes, ears, and minds.

Put on your armor today, my friend. A prepared soldier has a great chance of victory!

Suited in His armor,

Mikey

Christian soldiers wear the most important armor of all.

A Special Relationship

Introduction to Galatians

I remember when I first spotted the special young lady who is now my wife. My heart started twitterpating with innocent excitement over the little blonde with the blue flower in her hair. Her smile could warm up the coldest day, and her commitment to Christ was evident in every aspect of her life.

I wanted to meet her but didn't really know how. Over the weeks my mother began to notice my interest in this certain young lady as I carefully began asking questions about her. My parents were acquainted with her parents so I felt rather safe with the information they told me.

Then one day my mother told me that we were going to be sitting at the same table with the Pederson's at the annual church picnic! I was going to meet the little blonde with the blue flower in her hair! Life just seemed better than it ever had before.

The day soon arrived, and I was really nervous. I checked my hair as I went by each car on my way to the park. I remember saying hello to a lot of friends, but can't remember one of them. Finally, I reached the picnic table where we would eat. Soon others arrived and then I saw that special little blonde. She gracefully came up to the picnic table with her little sister, smiled and sat right across from me. I kicked my little brother in excitement.

The evening was wonderful. We spent most of it taking our younger brothers and sisters on the amusement park rides, but we did manage to get a few in together. I've never heard a girl scream so loud on a ferris wheel!

That September 8th evening a relationship began that would change both of our lives. We tried to spend every spare moment we could together so we could get to know each other better. I spoke with her parents for hours learning all that I could about this young lady. After three years, ten months and sixteen days, the little blonde with the blue flower in her hair walked down a long aisle to become my wife. Leesa still has that warm smile, and my heart will never be the same.

Getting to know someone takes time. Leesa and I wrote letters, talked on the phone, and even went through old baby books together. When you love someone, it is enjoyable learning about them.

You know, many of us are Christians but we take no time at all to learn about our Lord. We say we love the Lord, but rarely open the book that talks about His life. I learned a lot about Leesa because I spent time with her. The same is true for my relationship with the Lord Jesus. I need to spend time talking with the Lord and reading His love letter to me— the Bible. He wants to live through me if I'll only let Him. He wants to guide me through life if I'll only look at His road map.

I'm looking forward to meeting with you every day.

Your friend,

Mikey

★★ Day 58 ★★

Read Galatians 1:1–10   check here _____

DELIVERED

The battle seemed endless. For almost four years the North and South had been bombarding each other with cannons and gunfire. Men had become animals, hunting the enemy who wore blue or gray.

The five soldiers had somehow become separated from their company. Through the gunfire, they were forced to go east into the deep forest. They would hide out until nightfall and then try to rejoin their company.

As the last shades of sunlight fell behind the mountains, they slowly headed toward the ravine where their company had been. Coming over the crest, they looked down in shock to find their company completely destroyed. There, lying dead on the ground, were their friends and comrades. Fearing for their own lives, the five headed toward the river. Surely they could find some fellow soldiers there.

But enemy troops had invaded the river quarry. The five were spotted and a short battle broke out. Outnumbered, they soon surrendered to the enemy. Four of the five came out with hands raised behind their heads, but the fifth stayed perfectly still in the hollowed-out log he had been shooting from. For some reason the soldiers left the area unchecked and took their four prisoners away. Little did they know that one lay almost paralyzed in a log just a few steps away.

Fear gripped the four prisoners as they were gagged and taunted by their enemies. They were not fearful of the taunting but of what was ahead of them—the prison camp, a place of pain, horror, disease, and possible death.

For three long months the four prisoners endured the rat-infested prison and ill treatment. They were often beaten and given just bread and water to sustain strength, so it was not uncommon for a noisy rat to end up as an unexpected meal.

One night the prisoners were awakened by shooting. The shooting went on for hours, long into the next day. The prisoners could smell smoke from the nearby burning buildings. They wondered if they would burn to death or just waste away in their cell. Suddenly, the door came crashing **107** open, and there stood the one soldier who had stayed hidden in that hollow log. The prisoners had been delivered from a very real personal hell. One friend came back, risking his life to deliver many.

Look at verse 4 one more time and put a check here _____ after you have read it. Because of sin, an awful lot of bad stuff exists in this world we live in. Every day in the paper we can read of murder, dishonesty, rape, and sexual sin.

Are we going to always live in a world like this? The answer is in verse 4—no way. Jesus gave Himself for our sins to rescue us from the present world and its messes. Just like the friend in our story, so Jesus is coming again for us who know Him. Now that's hot news!

Rescued,

Mikey

Jesus is the only One who could set this captive free.

★★ Day 59 ★★

Read Galatians 1:11–24   check here _____

GOD'S BUSINESS: CHANGING LIVES

God is in the business of changing people's lives. No matter what we have done, we have a loving heavenly Father who is ready to forgive us and change us.

Paul, the writer of the four books of the Bible included in this devotional, was one bad dude! God changed his life to become one of the greatest examples of Christian faith. Do you know what Paul was doing before he became a Christian? Take a look at these verses and write down what Paul was like.

Galatians 1:13 _____

Galatians 1:23 _____

Acts 26:10–11 _____

Acts 22:20 _____

Paul was in the business of putting Christians to death

or in prison. He was a Christian bounty hunter of sorts! Now does it sound like this kind of person has a chance to be changed? Maybe not in our eyes, but no life is too dirty for God to change. Our heavenly Father can take a cruel man and turn him into a loving man. He can take a person full of hate and transform that person into someone full of joy. God can even take people like you and me and change us so we can be instruments that He can work through.

You may not have sin in your life to the degree that Paul did, but sin, no matter how little, separates us from God. If you haven't accepted Christ into your life, take the time and turn your life over to the Lord right now. He wants to come into your heart and change you as He did Paul.

Remember, we really are new creatures in Christ (2 Cor. 5:17).

Thankful for His change in me,

Mikey

God can make the impossible possible.

★★ Day 60 ★★

Read Galatians 2:1-10   **check here** _____

THE POOR ARE PEOPLE, TOO

As he got off the plane, he could not believe his eyes. Young children ran up to him with hands stretched out as far as they could reach. Those empty hands were begging for a mere penny or two which would be used to buy some rice. The sight of all those children made the pit of his stomach ache.

Later, as he entered a little village, he was greeted again with empty outstretched hands. He could not believe how these people lived. It was obvious that they were poor and undernourished.

Seeing poor people had always bothered this young man. But now he was having a different response to them. Instead of shying away or ignoring them, he began to smile at them and play with them. He began to see the real person inside the earthly shell. He saw these people laugh, run, cry, and hug each other. They were poor—but they were still people. That young man was I.

How do you respond to those with less than you? Do you ignore them or make fun of them? Do you think you are a better person because of the clothes in your closet or location of your home? We need to show that we care for all people regardless of what they wear or where they live. Paul says in verse 10 that he remembered the poor and he was eager to remember them. Write down four things that you could do for someone who is less fortunate than you.

1. _____

2. _____

3. _____

4. _____

Now pray for the chance to do them.

Loving all people with you,

Mikey

The poor are people, too!

★★ Day 61 ★★

Read Galatians 2:11–21   check here _____

Do you have a few favorite verses in the Bible? I do, too, and one of them is in today's reading. Can you guess which one it is? Well, if you guessed verse 20, you are absolutely right!

Please look at each phrase of that verse and write what it means to you.

"I have been crucified with Christ."

_____

"I no longer live but Christ lives in me."

_____

"The life I live in the body, I live by faith in the Son of God."

_____

"Who loved me and gave Himself up for me."

_____

Good job! Now you can see why this verse is so great. You have looked at it phrase-by-phrase and have put it in your own words. I'll look forward to meeting with you tomorrow, my friend!

Jesus is livin' in me, too,

Mikey

If Christ lives in you, you are one of God's kids.

★★ Day 62 ★★

Read Galatians 3:1–14   check here _____

Can you complete this puzzle today? All of the words are found in Galatians 3:1–14. Have fun and keep walking with Jesus, buddy!

Across

1. "Abraham believed God and it was credited to him as _____."
2. "The righteous will live by _____."
3. The name of this book.
4. Last word in verse 3.
5. Before their eyes Jesus was portrayed as _____.
6. Jesus performed many of these while on earth.

7. Another name for young human beings.
8. "All _____ will be blessed through you."
9. 37th word beginning with 3:1.

Down

1. 2nd word of verse 13.
2. "Are you so _____ ?"
3. You have 2 of them on your face.
4. You can cut trees with one.
5. His name appears 5 times.
6. In football a kicker can kick the ball for 3 points. It is called a field _____.
7. The first word of the quote in verse 10.
8. "Clearly no one is _____ by God through the Law."
9. 8th word in verse 14.
10. The Lord _____ Christ.

Meet me again here tomorrow.

Working by faith,

Mikey

When God seems far away, guess who moved?

Read Galatians 3:15–25   check here _____

PUTTING A GRANDPA FIRST

Old Jake never had a dog of his own. The shaggy visitor on the front porch made Jake's heart skip a little. He did not know where this golden labrador came from and hoped he would stay. So Jake pushed open the screen door and let his newfound friend inside the warm house.

After the dog's belly was full of freshly-baked biscuits, she sat at the feet of old Jake. A warm sensation swept through Jake's eighty-year-old body. He had found a special friend.

It didn't take Wilma long to discover Jake's new friend. She was cleaning the morning dishes when all of a sudden there appeared a four-legged creature. She laughed at the thought of seeing her husband of sixty years opening the door to let the dog in. Wilma put the table scraps on a plate, and they disappeared in seconds.

"You know you are going to have to put an ad in the town newspaper for that dog."

Jake was hoping Wilma would never say those words. He knew he had to do it, but he just didn't want to. The law required that you report a lost dog for three days in the town newspaper. So Jake made the shortest ad possible, which he hoped would go without notice:

> Dog Found
> Roshow Dr.

The first day that the ad came out it was way down at the bottom in the list of ads. Jake felt good about its location and was sure it would go unnoticed.

The second day Jake found the ad about halfway down the page. He still felt pretty good because it was well hidden.

But the third and final day, Jake found the ad on the very top of the page where everyone could see it. He didn't think much of it until later that night when there was a knock at his door. His heart sank at the sight of a young man in his twenties. Jake knew he was here to see the dog.

The young man and Jake sat and talked for quite a   *113*

while. The visitor could tell Jake was very warm toward his newfound friend. You could almost see the painful love in those old eyes. Jake's heart was aching as he thought about saying good-bye to the dog.

"What do you call her?" asked the young visitor.

"Well, I don't know her name, so I call her Friend," responded old Jake. He tried to hide the shakiness in his voice.

"Ya' know, you can always tell if a dog is yours by the way she responds to her name. Let me see if this dog is mine. Come here Lady, come here Lady."

The dog was sitting by the fire and slowly got up on her feet. Then she made her way past the visitor to the chair where old Jake was sitting. She sat down at his feet and gave a loving glance to the visitor.

"Nope, guess she isn't my dog," responded the boy with a snap in his voice. "I could have sworn that was Lady, but I guess I was wrong. Thank you for your time and keep trying for the right name. You will know when you get it right because a dog always responds to her name."

Then the visitor jumped into his truck and drove away in no time at all.

Jake smiled as Friend snuggled up beside him. He loved that look the dog gave him. Those big eyes just made him feel warm all over.

Jake didn't hear from anyone else about the dog. One day he received a strange telegram. There was no return person or address on it—just a message:

> For her name,
> try Brittany.

How are we to treat each other? _____

_____

What does it mean to look out for others' interests? ____

_____

Galatians 3:22 tells us there is a promise awaiting those who have named Jesus as their Lord and Savior. That promise is eternal life. Let's be sure we put others before
114 ourselves today!

Thinking of others,

Mikey

There is nothing more pitiful than a life spent thinking of nothing but self.

★★ **Day 64** ★★

Read Galatians 3:26–29   check here _____

THE FOREVER FAMILY

If you have received Jesus Christ into your life, then you are part of the greatest family of all time. It's a family where there will be equality, love, laughter, and unity. It's a family centered on the One who gave Himself up for all of us and made it possible for us to be together again. It's a family made up of some of the most famous people on earth and of the most poverty stricken on earth. It's a family that will last forever.

How does verse 26 say we become a son of God?

_____

_____

_____

Write down five people that you know are Christians. They can be sports stars, family members, friends, musicians, or even your pastor!

1. _____

2. _____

3. _____

4. _____

5. _____

These five people are special because they are part of God's family along with you. Can you imagine talking with Earl Campbell, Craig Morton, Billy Graham, Joshua, Paul, Amy Grant, Leon Patillo, and your best friend at the same table in heaven? I want to shoot baskets with Meadowlark Lemon or Julius Erving and play catch with Mike Davis. Wow! What a family! I want to meet those early Christians who died for their faith and my early Christian relatives. I want to see my Grandma Peterson again and laugh with her as we did before she died of cancer.

This family has hope. This family is unlike any other—it is warmer, friendlier, and more unified than any family on earth. Thank God today for being part of this special family.

Happy to be part of God's family,

Mikey

God's family will last forever!

★★ Day 65 ★★

Read Galatians 4:1–7   check here _____

ADOPTED AS GOD'S SONS

Justin was sitting on his bed in the slave quarters that he called home. Life was cruel in Rome. Just a few months ago, Justin had been the governor's son, going to the chariot races, the royal baths, and even the coliseum. But on that terrible night of the government overthrow, his father was beheaded in the town square. Justin was now no man's son and would be brought before the people on the trading block.

He would never forget the feeling as he had stood stripped and chained on the trading block. Men came by to look at him and talk to him a bit. Justin would go for a good price because he could read and write, and was strong for just fourteen years. It didn't take long to be sold. Justin was humiliated at the realization that he was a slave now, with a hole in his earlobe as proof.

His master was a kind man as far as masters go. Justin's job was to teach his master's niece to read and write. It was a good job for a slave to have and a lot easier than working the vineyards or olive groves. Over the years, Justin served his master well. He was soon promoted to the chieftain position, which was just under the master. He was to administer the crops, grounds, and his master's business. But there was one problem that remained—Justin was still a slave.

Then something happened that would change the course of Justin's life. His master had been gone for ten days on a trip to Galatia and returned talking about a man named Paul, who spoke about a man named Jesus. The master talked for hours, repeating the words of Paul and Jesus. Then he told how he had asked this Jesus into his own life and that now he would be living for Him.

These words astounded the slaves. Their master had clearly had a change of heart that would affect them all. Justin was to gather all the slaves together for a meeting, so the master could speak to them.

"My fellow slaves, you know that there has been a change in my life. I have made Jesus Christ, the Messiah, the Lord of my life. I hope for all of you to do the same someday, but that is up to you. Nothing will be forced upon you in this way. Paul spoke about freedom in Christ in such a way that it has touched my heart beyond words. I want to work things out with each of you, so that you will no longer be considered a slave. I will grant you your freedom and with that freedom you may choose to stay and work here or go out on your own."

The slaves were shocked. They were free. The master was giving them their freedom. How could this Jesus ever change a man like this? The slaves were jubilant as their master continued speaking.

"There is one who will be freed in a special way today. For years Justin has worked hard for me. He knows all about the business here and has done extremely well. He has become like a son to me, and I have become like a father to him. In my hand I hold a decree that states that Justin will become my adopted son if he so chooses. To accept, all 117

Justin has to do is take this decree from my hand."

Justin couldn't believe his ears—to be a man's son once again. All he had to do was take the decree. Everyone watched as Justin walked up the stairs, faced his master, and politely took the decree from his new father. The crowd cheered as Justin and his father clasped each other in a strong hug.

According to Galatians 4:5, have we been adopted as Justin was? _____

Write verse 6 in your own words. _____

_____

Write verse 7. _____

_____

We are sons of the living God. We were once slaves, but have been freed from the chains of sin and death by our Master, the Lord Jesus Christ. Have you thanked your heavenly Father today?

Jesus holds the keys that set us truly free.

★★ Day 66 ★★

Read Galatians 4:8–20   check here _____

Leesa leaned over and shook me gently. I thought she might be uncomfortable being a few days overdue, and then she said those words, "Mike, we need to get to the hospital."

Now we dads try to stay calm, cool, and collected at this moment but inside we are doing backflips. We know before long we are going to see our new baby.

We drove quickly to the hospital, and Leesa was hooked up to all kinds of electronic gizmos. Before long Leesa went into contractions, and the birth process began.

Oh my, I sure am glad God made me a man. I understand why they call it labor now. The pain is excruciating but the reward is so precious. "Katie and Michael are worth every bit of pain," Leesa said afterward.

What does Paul say about childbirth pains in verse 19?

Yes, he is actually in labor for them. In other words, He's workin' hard to see them grow.

Who are the people in your life workin' hard to see you grow? Your parents, youth minister, friend, or even me? Jot down two names of those who labor to make life easier for you.

1. _____

2. _____

Laboring to see you grow,

Mikey

All the joys of life have their price.

★★ Day 67 ★★

Read Galatians 4:21–31   check here _____

SPECIAL IN GOD'S EYES

Many years ago, in a small midwest town, before the west was won, there lived a little family. They had a humble home, which looked more like a cabin than a house. They made a modest living by farming wheat and corn. Inside, the mother had just given birth to a little boy. He was only moments old, but so complete. He had all his fingers, all of his toes, and a beautiful smile. His little eyes danced like diamonds, and his sandy-colored hair seemed to glow in the sunlight. He certainly was a precious child.

Over the months little Jimmy began to grow. His body was getting bigger, and his movements were becoming more defined. It was getting difficult to confine this little "creepy crawler" to one room. He seemed to always have something on his mind and somewhere to go.

As Jimmy continued to grow, his mom and dad detected a problem. Their child was very quiet and almost acted as if no one else was in the room at times. Mom and Dad knew something wasn't just right, so they went to see Doc.

It didn't take Doc long to detect the problem. Jimmy was deaf. He grew up in his silent world doing the daily chores he had been shown how to do. He was a strong boy and a good worker. The only way his parents knew how to communicate with him was by facial expressions and showing him how something had to be done.

One day his mom and dad heard of a man in the next town who somehow spoke with his hands. They didn't understand this "sign language" but decided to take Jimmy to the "hand man." It only took Jimmy six months to master the new language. But one day stood out from all the others. It was on this day that the hand man explained who Jesus was and how Jesus died on the cross for his sins. Soon Jimmy asked the Savior into his life. He was a different person now, with a new view on life. He returned home and taught this sign language to his parents so they could communicate with him.

Jimmy continued to grow up and soon started a school for the deaf where the students would live and learn how to communicate in the silent world. Before long there were more students than he could handle, so he began a second school in the next town.

By the end of Jimmy's long life, hundreds of schools for the deaf were started, and thousands of kids made Jesus their Lord and Savior. He never gave up on life nor the God who made him so special.

God made Jimmy just how He wanted him. There was no mistake and his effective life proved that. In the same way, God did not make a mistake when He made you. He knew exactly what He was doing. He created you into a very special human being and longs to draw close to you through His Son Jesus Christ. Just how special are you? Come on— let's take a look in God's love letter to you.

Turn to Psalm 139 (in the middle of your Bible). Write down three things that God knows about you that are found in Psalm 139:1—6 (they are really easy to find!).

1. _____

2. _____

3. _____

Did you know God knows you better than you know yourself? He even knows your thoughts and desires. God loves you just the way you are. That's why He made you like He did.

Now look at Psalm 139:13—16 and put these verses into your own words. Just jot down what these verses mean to you. (I know you can do it—just try.)

1. Ps. 139:13 _____

2. Ps. 139:15 _____

3. Ps. 139:16 _____

God made us and He knows us. We can really be thankful for that. You have been made by God and are very precious in His sight. He loves you just the way you are, and don't forget it!

Thankful for how God made me,

Mikey

God knew what He was doing when He made you!   **121**

FREE TO SIN NO MORE

Golathan was the most feared slave master in Tritan. His slaves were chained by hand and by foot as well as by yoke, placed around each slave's neck. The hot humid weather in Tritan made the slaves skin glisten with sweat as they labored all day long in their chains.

To be a slave of Golathan meant more than just chains. It meant that you were a slave to a lifestyle not fit for any human being. This lifestyle was hard, cruel, and eventually ended in a gruesome death.

Now King Reneir was a respectable and very kind man. He was king of the entire area except for Golathan's territory. He had just heard of Golathan and his cruel ways of life. He knew that he must somehow find a way to free Golathan's slaves.

One night, as Golathan and his men were sleeping, King Reneir and his army quietly crept over the large stone walls. They made their way to the slaves quarters and soon found hundreds eager to be released. Their chains made it impossible to leave quietly, so King Reneir took a key out of his dark coat. What a beautiful "click" each of the slaves heard as their chains hit the ground. Each slave was helped over the wall and sent to King Reneir's castle for protection.

The next morning, a very angry Golathan and his men stood at the drawbridge of the castle.

"Where are my slaves?" screamed Golathan.

King Reneir appeared and answered Golathan's angry

voice.

"The slaves are slaves no longer. They have been set free by me and my men. You may return to your territory, but beware, if I hear of your treating slaves as such again I will take your head."

Golathan and his men turned and rode back to their homes in disgust. The former slaves cheered joyfully. They were truly free.

About a week later, the king was checking on the former slaves to see how they were doing. To his surprise he saw several of them being as cruel as their old master to others. He noticed them screaming and carrying on just as they did in their chains. Shocked at this, the king called a meeting for all the former slaves. All of them came and heard these words that they would never forget.

"My friends, weeks ago my men and I risked our lives to rescue you from your yoke of slavery. We released you from your chains and brought you to a safe territory. We gave you your complete freedom. You are free men and women. But as I walked among you today, I found that you are not really free at all. You are still slaves because you are as mean and cruel as your old master. Your chains are off, but you are shackled by cursing, cheating, and fighting. To be really free, you must put these things behind you. Why go back to these evil ways and enslave yourselves again? Free yourselves! You were set free so you could exercise your freedom. Now go and live as truly free men and women."

With heads lowered, the free people understood their failure. The chains were gone, but they had made themselves slaves to their old habits. They all left that night different people. They were free now, and they were going to live like it.

How does this story relate to you as a Christian? _____

_____

Are there some habits that are hanging on to you? If so, give them to the Lord right now, my friend.

Free to sin no more,

Mikey

We were set free, so give Jesus the ball and chain.   **123**

Read Galatians 5:2–15   check here _____

I'll never forget watching the newsclips that evening. It was the dead of winter, and a plane had just crashed into the freezing waters of the Potomac river. The plane was slowly sinking through the ice, and the helpless people in the water hung onto whatever they could to remain afloat. Within minutes a rescue helicopter was in sight. An unidentified man began to help others onto the seat of the helicopter. The seat was attached to long ropes, and the helicopter pulled the people one by one to the frozen shore.

The man in the water continued to help others onto the helicopter seat instead of jumping onto the seat himself. Finally, his turn had come. But as the helicopter returned to rescue this soon-to-be hero, they found no one. The helicopter made several passes until finally, they had to give up their search. This man was so busy helping others that he failed to recognize his own life-threatening situation—his limbs were freezing. He hung on as long as possible, but before the helicopter could return, this man became another victim. The hearts of the world were touched by the love and giving spirit of that fellow human being. I, for one, have never forgotten those newsclips of the man who gave his life for others.

In verse 14 it says the law is summed up in one command. What is that command? _____

_____

_____

What does Matthew 22:39 say? _____

_____

_____

Now write down two ways you can really show love to your neighbor today.

1. _____

124   2. _____

Keep up the great work, my friend. We still have a few more days left together. I'll talk to you tomorrow.

Living to give my life away,

Mikey

Love your neighbor as yourself.

★★ Day 70 ★★

Read Galatians 5:16–18

check here _____

During lunch time at the local middle school, everyone seemed to be huddled into their own little groups. It was sure nice to talk to your friends and give your mind a short vacation from thinking so hard in class, a relaxing time. That is, until Gordon came around.

"Say, did you guys see me at the game last night? I scored the most points. Boy, I sure did good on that test last hour in history, too. I can't wait 'til school is over so I can go visit my dad in Hollywood." And on and on.

You see, Gordon never stopped talking about himself. He felt like he was God's gift to the human race. When Gordon came, we spent the rest of our time listening to Gordon talk about Gordon!

Have you ever met a person like Gordon? People like him can drive you nuts! A self-centered person is concerned only with himself and his own accomplishments. We all tend to get a bit like this at times, don't we?

Galatians 5:16 says to live by the what? _____

To live by the Spirit means to be others-centered, instead of self-centered. How many times does the word "Spirit" appear in verses 16—18? _____

Let's be careful about being self-centered, my friends. Instead, let's be "others-centered."

Thinking of others,

Mikey

An egotist is an "I" specialist.

★★ **Day 71** ★★

Read Galatians 5:19—26   check here _____

Hey guys, let's check out the differences in the acts of the sinful nature and the fruits of the Spirit. They should be really obvious because they are opposite of each other.

Acts of the sinful nature   *Fruit of the Spirit*

1. _____   1. _____

2. _____   2. _____

3. _____   3. _____

4. _____   4. _____

5. _____   5. _____

6. _____   6. _____

7. _____   7. _____

8. _____   8. _____

9. _____   9. _____

10. _____

11. _____

12. _____

13. _____

14. _____

15. _____

Which side do you want to be more like? I don't know about you, but I want to be on that right side. In fact, put a check next to one of those qualities you can work on today. You are special to me. I'll meet with you tomorrow, my friend.

Living in the Spirit,

Mikey

The acts of the sinful nature and the fruit of the Spirit are opposites that will never attract.

★★ **Day 72** ★★

Read Galatians 6:1–5   check here _____

DOING YOUR BEST

They always told him he was going to be a great athlete when he grew a few more inches. Deep inside, he knew those inches would probably never come. He stood just 5'4", but he could be seen shooting baskets in his driveway until the sun went down. Every spare moment was spent shooting baskets and running around a basketball court.

In junior high, he continued to play as often as possible. He was never great, but contributed to the team each game. In high school, he continued to play and do the best with what God had given him. During his senior year in high school, he was selected to represent Jesus Christ on a basketball team to the Philippines.

This person was never a great star. He was consistent in his desire and longed to do the very best with what God had blessed him with. Yes, he was small, but he did not let his height deter him. Instead he made up his mind to do the best he could do. You see, I know this person very well—it is I.

God does not ask us to make all-star teams, honor societies, or be top finishers in a beauty contest to be of use to Him. No way. God just asks us to give back to Him what He has given us. He asks us to do the very best we can and be happy with it. He doesn't want us comparing ourselves with others and walking around feeling lousy because we didn't do as well as someone else. He just wants us to be ourselves!

Today, write down verse 4 in your own words. _____

_____

_____

_____

_____

_____

Now write down three areas where you want to do your best for the Lord.

1. _____

2. _____

3. _____

You are great just the way you are. God wants to use you, and He will if you let Him. If He can work through someone who is 5'4'', then I know He can work through you, too!

Enjoying how God made me,

Mikey

When we compare ourselves with others, it's easy to feel bad about ourselves.

Read Galatians 6:6–10   check here _____

Dawn came home from her first-grade class full of excitement. She had just been taught how to mold clay, and she marveled at the funny-looking lump that sat on the table.

"I've never seen such a nice piece of clay," responded Dawn's mother as only a mother could do. "That piece of clay sure is special."

Dawn smiled as her mother graciously complimented her several times.

"Mommy, do you know what I am going to do?"

"No, Dawn, tell me.

"I am going to make a clay doggie for my daddy because he likes doggies."

Dawn then took her little piece of clay and bounced off to her room. It would take some time to make such a nice present for her dad.

Dawn's door was closed all afternoon as her little fingers molded the clay into four legs and the body of a dog. Her mom was happy, realizing how serious Dawn was in doing something good for her father.

When Dad came home, he was not allowed in Dawn's room. At dinner, Dawn would talk and then smile at him. She felt so good inside that you could read it on her face.

When dinner was over, Dawn hurried back to her room to resume the work on her masterpiece. Finally, just before bedtime, Dawn entered the room where her dad was sitting with something hidden behind her back.

"Daddy, I made something for you, and I did it all by myself." Dawn glowed with pride. "This doggie is for you, Daddy, because I know that you like doggies."

She brought the little clay figure out from behind her back and proudly put it in her father's hands. "This doggie is for you, Daddy. I made it for you."

Dad grabbed his little girl and gave her a big hug. He told her how nice it looked and how happy he was to know that she had made it for him.

Later that night, Dad set the piece of clay on his dresser. To anyone else the piece of clay resembled more of a cow than a dog and belonged in the garbage can. But to **129**

Dad it was a masterpiece because his little girl made it just for him. He slept well that night, knowing his little girl had done something very good for him—too good for words to explain.

When was the last time you did something good for another person? If you can't remember, then I think it's time to take care of it.

What does verse 9 say about doing good? _____

_____

How about verse 10? _____

_____

_____

When we do good things for others, it truly honors God. Write down two things that you could do tomorrow.

1. _____

2. _____

Now do them, my friend!

Doing good with you,

Mikey

You haven't begun to give until you feel good about it!

★★ **Day 74** ★★

Read Galatians 6:11–15   **check here** _____

Well, my friend, we just have today and tomorrow left. I want to thank you for meeting with me each day. You really are special to me, and I want you to know that.

Friends are special people and that is what you are to me, my friend. I may not have met you yet but I sure hope to some day. If you are a Christian, then I know for sure I'll see you.

One of my favorite Christian artists is Michael W. Smith. He sings a song entitled "Friends." Here are a few of the words.

And friends are friends forever
If the Lord's the Lord of them
And a friend will not say never
'Cause a welcome will not end
Though it's hard to let you go
In the Father's hands we know
That a lifetime's not too long
To live as friends.

Now take a look at these verses and put a star by the one you like the best.

Proverbs 17:17   John 15:13
Proverbs 18:24   1 Samuel 20:17

Now, write down one name of someone who is a close friend of yours. _____ If you can't think of anyone, then remember me!

Your friend forever,

Mikey

Friends are friends forever, if the Lord's the Lord of them.

★★ **Day 75** ★★

BRAND-NAME CHRISTIANS

Guess what? We got the title for this book from this last little passage of Scripture. Paul said, "I bear on my body the marks of Jesus." Paul actually had physical scars for standing up for Jesus Christ. Those scars reminded him who he belonged to—he was the Lord's property and he knew it.

Read 2 Corinthians 11:23–27 to see what scars Paul might have had on his body. Write down 2 of them:

1. _____

2. _____

So what about us? We aren't beaten or shipwrecked very often, so we probably don't have physical scars on our bodies to remind us of times we stood up for Christ. Those scars, in a sense, were Paul's brand-name label—they told who he belonged to. But what kind of brand-name label would those scars have been if they hadn't been backed up by a Christian life and attitudes?

What are some of the marks of a brand-name Christian? I think one might be a joyful spirit and a warm smile; another, a person who opens God's Word daily and has a consistent prayer life; and another, someone who shares faith in Christ with a friend.

Can you think of three others?

1. _____

2. _____

3. _____

Those "brand-name labels" may be the things that tell the world we belong to Jesus Christ. But we don't really need those labels to tell ourselves who we belong to, do we? After all, we have God's Word that assures us and reminds us that we are His.

A brand-name Christian spends time in God's Word. If you have spent time with this book and an open Bible for the

past few weeks, then you *are* a brand-name Christian—and

I'm really proud of you. Hold your head high and continue to keep yourself in God's Word. I've enjoyed every day with you, and I want you to know that I love you,

I'm a Brand-Name Christian,

Mikey

Brand-name Christians are Christians who spend time with their Savior.